T0315911

NOTTINGHAM
versus
NAPOLEON

MICHAEL P. KIRKBY

NOTTINGHAM
versus
NAPOLEON

The story of an English County's
defiance of an Empire

First published 2016 by DB Publishing, an imprint of JMD Media Ltd,
Nottingham, United Kingdom.

ISBN 978-1-78091-536-4

Copyright © Michael P. Kirkby

All Rights Reserved. No part of this publication may be reproduced, stored in a retrieval
system, or transmitted in any form, or by any means, electronic, mechanical, photocopying,
recording or otherwise without the prior permission in writing of the copyright holders,
nor be otherwise circulated in any form or binding or cover other than in which it is
published and without a similar condition being imposed on the subsequent publisher.

Printed and bound in the UK by Copytech (UK) Ltd Peterborough

INTRODUCTION

On the evening of 18 June 1815, Arthur Wellesley, The Duke of Wellington, wearily rode to his quarters, lay down and slept. Just a few hours before, the combined army of British, Dutch and Germans under his command and their Prussian Allies had defeated the French army under the command of the Emperor, Napoleon Bonaparte on the field of Waterloo, a tiny Belgian hamlet, thus permanently securing the future of Europe.

Unbeknownst to Wellington, this was to be the last time France and Britain would face each other as enemies on the field and a new Europe was to be forged. The vast French empire that had stretched from the West Indies, Africa, Europe and the East was now in tatters, it's feared Emperor was on the run trying to reassemble what was left of his army and his generals had all abandoned him.

From 1792 Britain and the major powers of Europe had been in a succession of coalitions against Revolutionary France, often trading allies for enemies. Whilst their navies clashed on the high seas for control of the trade routes their armies weren't to engage until 1800 when both Britain and France sought control of Egypt ending with a British victory. After the French invasion of Spain in 1808, Britain moved to take action and an army was pieced together and shipped over to break France's strangle hold over Europe. This expeditionary force was to remain on the continent for seven years fighting the French in the harsh Portuguese mountains, the vast Spanish plains and eventually push them back into France in what was to later become termed as The Peninsula War.

The Peninsula War was more than just a series of conflicts in a foreign country. It was to be the making of the career of many British generals, it was to be a time of innovation and revolutionary development in the armed forces, and mostly it was going to be the test of British mettle against overwhelming numbers.

Within the ranks of this small, ill-prepared expeditionary force were Nottinghamshire men. Weavers, farmers, labourers, carpenters, tradesmen and many more from the heart of the midlands were to see conflict on foreign battlefields. Both of the county's regiments the 45th (1st Nottinghamshire) and 59th (2nd Nottinghamshire) were to come face-to-face repeatedly against the French war machine and fight in some of the most decisive battles of that era. There were many more men who joined to fight with other infantry units, some who joined the cavalry, others the artillery and some in support units who all hailed from the county to combat the French threat.

This is the story of how the local regiments and local individuals witnessed one of the last great European wars before the age of mechanised warfare, in an age where cavalry charged and infantry marched. This is the story of Nottingham versus Napoleon.

FEVER AND FATIGUE

The Indies and South America

When the French Republic formally declared war on the First Coalition in 1793 the 45th were stationed in the West Indies trying to secure and protect British trade routes to the New World from their European competitors. The 45th and the French began to conflict in small engagements in a bid to clear the islands of their opposition.

Cholera, dysentery and tropical fevers such as Yellow Fever were rife in the Indies. Contracted from mosquito bites, symptoms were shivering, nausea and pain, followed by the yellowing of the skin (hence the name) and ultimately death. Yellow Fever had such an impact in the ranks of the 45th that by 1794, the Regiment that had set out with near to one thousand officers and men was reduced to a paltry five officers and 71 men. The tropical diseases were so debilitating that in 1787 it was recorded that the average number of casualties ranged from nine to 14, out of a total number of 340 men making the entire regiment.

After a brief stint in England to recruit their massively depleted ranks the 45th went back to the West Indies with 686 officers and men in total.

During the 45th's second term in the Indies from 1795–1802 they had very little contact with the French, but did succeed in pushing the French out of Dominica, Martinique and Iles des Saints, and instead garrisoned the trading posts and forts. This came at a heavy loss, as between 1797–98 13 officers died of disease, including the commanding officer Lt Col Frazer, combined with other ranks this left the regiment totalling 356 men in 1799. The 45th did manage to recruit volunteers in 1800 bringing the strength back up merely to 407 all ranks but in 1802, they were eventually ordered to Ireland to recuperate and recruit in face of the ever-growing European threat of French expansion and invasion. Despite the horrific conditions and terrible climate, surprisingly 202 men of the Regiment volunteered to remain in the West Indies and transferred themselves to other Regiments.

The 45th had very little time to rebuild its strength in Ireland. In August 1806, the 45th were sent as part of General John Whitelock's force to South America to recapture the important trading town of

Buenos Aires, which had fallen back to the Spanish in 1805. Serving in General Caitlin Craufurd's brigade, the objectives of the 45th were to; '…capture the seaports and fortresses and the reduction of the Province of Chili.'

After nine months at sea the British forces finally landed at Montevideo on 14 June 1807. Though the months at sea had been extremely difficult, with many units losing complete order and discipline, the 45th, aboard their troop transport *Fame*, maintained such high standards and discipline that officers from other regiments were instructed to go aboard and seek council from their commander, Major Gwyn, on how to maintain an orderly regiment in such conditions.

On 3 July Whitelock's forces converged upon Buenos Aires with Craufurd's brigade on the right flank. The plan was that the force would attack the town in eight columns and fan out pushing the defenders back towards the River Plate. However, Buenos Aires was typical of all Spanish towns of this period. It was designed on a street grid of major roads with side streets all at right angles branching off and connecting to other roads. All of the buildings were quite high with flat roofs enabling defenders to pour down a deathly fire upon any attackers. Further still, in order to prevent the British troops from firing into each other, it was ordered that the troops march with un-loaded weapons to prevent any accidents occurring.

On 5 July, the 45th were to hold the extreme right and were to attack in two wings. The first commanded by Lt. Col. William Guard, and the other by Major Nicholls. Their aim was to take the Residencia des Barbones and hold it until all forces could converge together.

Col. Guard, along with the Grenadier Company detoured whilst advancing to reconnoitre with Gen. Craufurd but found themselves amongst the back alleyways surrounded by enemy troops who were holding the rooftops. Nicholls made it as far as his objective and secured the Residencia. In doing so he deployed two companies towards the River Chuelo to prevent an attack and then dispatched the rest of his companies to secure the surrounding buildings, in doing so he succeeded in capturing prisoners and two cannons.

However, elsewhere the battle was not going in the British favour. The 88th Foot, who had the honour of attacking the centre found themselves surrendering to the overwhelming fire from the Spanish held positions. Col. Guard and the Grenadiers took shelter in the Convent but heavy enemy fire, combined with Craufurd's refusal to surrender, brought more fire upon them. Only at 4pm did Craufurd reluctantly hoist the white flag of truce, but it had cost Guard 40 of his men wounded or killed.

The British retreated back to the edge of the town with their own prisoners leaving those trapped to the mercy of the Spanish.

However, the next day the Spanish Commander, General Liviers, sent a note to Whitelock promising a return of all prisoners if the British embark and leave at once. Whitelock requested 24 hours to think it over but on the seventh he agreed to Liviers terms.

Despite the bitter defeat, the 45th had achieved their goals and Nicholls had created quite an impact that would go on to affect his future with the army. Upon the capture of the two cannons Whitelock had told him, *'Nicholls, I am highly obliged to you for your exertions...I shall mention you in Orders, as well as in the despatch.'* As good as his word, Whitelock spoke very generously of the 45th and Nicholls in his despatch, gladly stating; *'Nor should I omit the gallant conduct of Major Nicholls of the 45th Regiment, who, on the morning of the 6th, being pressed by the enemy near to the Residencia, charged them with great spirit and took two howitzers and many prisoners.'*

The other Generals in command of the expedition had also come to hear of Nicholls' exploits, with General Leveson Gower commenting *'...you have completely established the reputation of the regiment, and your own.'* And General Sir Samuel Auchmuty claiming that *'had all the posts been maintained as yours, the town must have been ours.'*

The 45th marched out of Buenos Aires with flags flying and heads held high, knowing that they did all they could, given the circumstances. However, the price of Nicholls' achievements had been 14 killed, 44 wounded including three officers and one missing. Other side effects were also a sudden rise in desertion rates as the Spanish never properly returned the men to their regiments, but merely told them they were free and left them to it, others literally encouraged men to desert their regiments. In doing so many men opted to remain or merely disappeared into the South American undergrowth. Nicholls' adventure in South America still had one more twist of fate to make. Having embarked with the 45th on 12–13 July, he was requested by Whitelock to return to Buenos Aires as a Spanish hostage as both sides had agreed to keep three of the enemy officers to ensure peace was kept. However, Nicholls, arriving back, found this had fortunately been reduced to only one hostage and he was allowed to return to his Regiment. Arriving back in Ireland in December 1807, Nicholls was gazetted to a higher rank in another regiment but continued a long and distinguished career.

The 59th (2nd Nottinghamshire) Regiment followed an almost similar route as their sister regiment in the build up to the war with Napoleonic France. In 1793 the regiment was dispatched to Flanders to deter the French forces gathering there from threatening the allied supply depot at Ostend. In June the following year they disembarked at Ostend as part of the Duke of York's infamous and later, disastrous, expedition into Holland. Overwhelming French forces defeated the Duke's army at Fleurus and the 59th took part in a long retreat on Ghent, Bruges and Mechelen. By November of the same year the 59th were under siege at Nijmegen. When Nijmegen fell the 59th fell back over the River Waal into the Dutch United Provinces.

Their ordeal was not over and in January 1795 the 59th found their position being attacked by a whole French division and had no choice but to hold their ground for over two hours, losing fifty men in the process. Holding back the French attack, the 59th continued its march north and in March 1795 they embarked at Bremen for home. The Duke of York's Holland expedition had been a complete disaster but became immortalised forever in the popular children's song *The Grand Old Duke of York*. His marching of troops to the top of the hill and down again satirises the aging Duke's inability to make strategic decisions.

In the summer of 1795 the 59th were sent to St Vincent in the Indies where the black Caribs, under encouragement from the French, were rising up against the British. On 2 October the 59th engaged the Caribs at their stronghold and though initially they couldn't shift them, they managed to progress further onto their position when the Caribs withdrew in the evening. However, the Caribs regrouped and attacked the main British fort and battery causing the British to retreat to Kingstown, a retreat that would have seen more casualties had the two hundred men of the 59th under Colonel Fuller not held off the Carib advance allowing the rest of the army to retreat.

Fresh troops were brought to the Caribbean under Sir Ralph Abercrombie where the British counter attacked and caught the Carib force on three sides and broke their rebellion. With the Caribs now back under British control the 59th left St Vincent in July and their force split over St Kitts and Antigua for the next six years on garrison duty. Similarly to the 45th their ranks were thinned greatly due to fever and tropical illness rather than enemy action.

The 59th was recalled to England in July 1802 to recruit and rebuild its heavily depleted ranks. Their service in the Indies was so well behaved that The House of Assembly in Antigua requested 200 guineas be sent ahead to London to purchase silver plate for the regimental mess.

Arriving back in England in July 1802 the regiment was stationed on the South East coast on garrison duty in preparation for a French invasion. In 1804 as a renewed war with Napoleonic France loomed ever closer Whitehall instructed the regiment to raise a second battalion and in November that year twenty NCO's went to Chesterfield to begin recruiting from militias and the public. By April the following year the regiment, now back to full strength embarked at Gosport to be posted to India.

THE FIRST INVASION
OF THE IBERIA

Rolica – Vimiero – Retreat to Corruna

Whilst on their way to India in 1807 the 59th stopped off in Brazil, then a Portuguese colony, for repairs to be made to their transport ships. Whilst here France launched an invasion of their old ally Spain and her neighbour Portugal in a bid to push home their European blockade of Great Britain completely.

The young Arthur Wellesley, serving in Ireland, had been preparing to sail to South America with a force of 9,000 men to reinforce Whitelock's troops already there. However, the French invasion of Spain ultimately altered his plans and instead he found himself sailing for Mondego Bay, Portugal where a further 5,000 troops under Sir Brent Spencer were to reinforce him.

Like many other British regiments, both the 1/45th and the 2/59th were redirected from their duties abroad and despatched to the Iberian Peninsula to resist the French invader. Thus, the 45th, numbering 35 officers, 38 sergeants, 37 corporals, 22 drums and 635 privates, on their way back to England after the disastrous expedition to Buenos Aires, never made it as far as English soil, owing to the fact they were re-directed to Spain from Ireland in July 1808 although official records of the time at the outbreak of the invasion of Spain denote that the 45th comprised of 1,610 men with the first battalion making up the Peninsular Field Army and it's second battalion at home.

The expedition was placed under the overall command of Sir Hew Dalrymple and his second-in-command Lt. General Sir Harry Burrard. The expedition was to land in two ports. The main army consisting of the 45th under the command of Dalrymple was to take Mondego Bay and a further 12,000 troops with which the 2/59th served, under the command of Sir David Baird, was to land at Corruna in north-west Spain. The plan was that both armies would march inland and secure a foothold then meet up to face the French.

Wellesley reached Oporto on 25 July, replenished his forces, and then re-embarked for Mondego Bay where he could march directly on Lisbon. Reaching Mondego Bay on 30 July 1808, the troop transports moored off the coast in preparation for their European invasion. On 1 August the first troops disembarked and landed at Mondego Bay. It would be another four days before Brent Spencer arrived with his force of 5,000.

The 45th, serving in Brigadier Caitlin Crauford's 5th brigade, were amongst the first of the 14,000 Wellesley/Brent Spencer force to disembark along with Wellesley and immediately marched towards the village of Leira, to seize an important junction. Wellesley's orders from London decreed that once he had a sufficient force at his disposal he was to secure Mondego Bay and press on into Portugal to reconnoitre the area until he could be reinforced.

Wellesley's force of 14,000 men, almost all infantry, was engaged almost immediately with French General de la Borde's forces. On 17 August at Rolica Ridge, de la Borde made a stand on the Lisbon Road in hope that his outnumbered force could hold the British advance until Marshal Junot's force, only a few hours away, could reach him in time. The 45th plus Light Companies from other regiments, held the extreme left, opened the battle by driving the French from the road running straight through de la Borde's positions. The first of the 45th's casualties were attained in the opening battle when French artillery targeted the Colour Parties, successfully hitting Ensign Dawson, carrying the King's Colours and cutting the Staff of the Regimental Colours in half. Other casualties taken were those of Lt. Burke and nine other ranks.

Bolstered by a further 1,700 Portuguese troops, Wellesley threw his men forward in a flanking movement around the ridge and pressured De la Borde into turning his forces. De la Borde, at risk of becoming trapped between two forces, made a hasty retreat at the cost of 600 men to Wellesley's 474 casualties.

Wellesley had succeeded in drawing first blood for the British against the French invader and had now set a bar that would be difficult to better. Despite his victory, Wellesley hastily camped at Rolica in face of a fresh French assault under Junot, who was not too far away and sent for 4,000 reinforcements. Wellesley was ordered by Burrard to Vimiero where he was to make a line of defence, in order to cover the rest of the disembarking troops which took place on 18, 19 and 20 August. Wellington, as one of the more junior Generals in this expedition, was eager to move on Junot in order to demonstrate his competency to his superior officers. Burrard however, was cautious and would not allow any further actions until Sir John Moore had arrived with his troops.

Wellesley, who had gone back to Vimiero, hurriedly organized his troops in expectation of an attack from the south. On the morning of 21 August, the French approached as anticipated, but from the east. Wellesley hurriedly issued new orders to avoid being flanked and utilising the landscape to his advantage; he positioned his troops on the ridges and hills around Vimiero.

Lacking any substantial artillery or cavalry, Wellington's only chance to even out the odds was to position his troops in a manner that allowed the enemy to march onto him exposing themselves.

Wellesley, expecting an attack from the south, had five brigades positioned on a ridge ready to engage Junot's forces. He was forced to move three of these hurriedly, to reinforce the attack now approaching from his east. The 45th were kept as part of the reserve behind the east ridge in a bid to deter any flanking movement by the French onto the rear of the army.

Junot, opening with an artillery bombardment, sent his forces in three columns to attack Wellesley's weak left flank, right at east Ridge, and centre (Vimiero Hill), simultaneously.

First, Wellesley threw forward a skirmish line to tie up the French *voltigeurs*, light Infantrymen who would run ahead of the main column to try and distract the British fire and also to try inflict as many casualties in the British line as possible through pot-shots in anticipation for the main French attack.

Next as the massed French ranks pushed onto the British positions, Wellesley's skirmish line broke and lured the French to the top of the crest where just behind, the main body of troops were well formed to pour disciplined and massed volley fire into the French ranks, who, due to their massed ranks, were unable to properly return fire at the British infantry.

One by one, Junot's columns began to weaken, break and flee in the face of the British Infantry. Wellesley ordered a cavalry charge to harass the fleeing French, but they overstretched themselves and found they were riding with the fugitive French not into them. The cavalry suffered many casualties as they had no sufficient artillery support to cover them.

Completely astounded, Junot limped away, planning a tactical retreat where he could regroup his troops and reinforcements and plan another attack. Wellesley, keen to push home his victory had the problem of convincing Burrard to pursue the fleeing Junot, and break his forces completely. However, Burrard delayed as he was still awaiting the arrival of Sir John Moore and his force in the Peninsula.

On 22 August, Sir Hew Dalrymple came ashore and Wellesley tried to persuade him to let him pursue Junot who was slipping away. Dalrymple was even more obstinate than Burrard and would not allow a pursuit. That afternoon, French General Kellerman came to the British lines proposing a truce. Junot was willing to quit Portugal if he could take his men with him.

Dalrymple agreed to a weeks truce whilst they try to organize troops and draw up a treaty. In this time, Wellesley strongly maintained that the British were capable of defeating Junot's forces and should attack without delay. Unfortunately, both of his superior officers seemed keen to make a truce and on 1 September, the British moved their HQ to Cintra, near Lisbon, to draw up a treaty with the French. The following treaty became known as the Convention of Cintra and was to shake up the army hierarchy in the Peninsula. In return for their co-operation, forts, stores and arsenals, the French could safely remain in Lisbon until the British could find enough transport ships to take them to France. However, this arrangement caused massive upset with the Portuguese who refused to feed, clothe, and provide for their new guests and developed a suspicion of where British allegiances actually lay. They began to mock their British liberators and some merchants even refused to trade with the British Army.

Meanwhile the 45th were ordered to Torres Vedras where they were to protect the main Lisbon supply line where a force under Capt. Greenwell succeeded in securing the Fortress of Peniche from the French garrison.

On 24 September, Moore finally came ashore to find a very volatile situation ready to erupt at any moment. Worse still, news of the Treaty had reached London and politicians back home were calling for an explanation as to why this situation had got out of hand. Within due course, Dalrymple, Burrard and Wellesley were recalled to England to face a Court of Enquiry, leaving Sir John Moore, who had already missed the first two engagements of the Peninsula War, to repair the damage caused by his commanders.

Moore, with a meagre 20,000 men at his disposal, attempted to march from Lisbon into Spain, in the hope that he could meet up with General Sir David Baird arriving from England to Corruna, there to march on Madrid, with a further 10,000 men before Moore must engage the French. However, the Spanish authorities refused Baird permission to land at Corruna in the time Moore needed his assistance and only on 12 October 1808, by which time Moore had already marched on, was Baird allowed to disembark his force consisting of 12,000 men inclusive of the 2/59th.

Moore, preparing to advance into enemy territory requested Craddock to send him more troops in the form of the 82nd and 97th, and the 45th were to form the garrison at Almeida as well as being spread over Lisbon, Oporto and Lanergo.

Moore split his forces and advanced with the bulk of the Infantry over the inhospitable, yet shorter routes through the mountain passes, whilst sending his artillery and cavalry under the command of Sir John Hope, a longer route on more stable terrain. Baird's army, now fully disembarked marched to Santiago de Compostela and turned east to Lugo with the intention to join up with Moore's force in Portugal.

In early November Moore crossed the River Tagus at Villa Velha with close to 30,000 men under his command. However, Moore's men were scattered in three divisions over a 100-mile area and though his Spanish allies had 100,000 men, they were poorly trained, ill-disciplined and tied up holding Marshal Jourdan's 70,000 French at the River Ebro.

On 5 November, Napoleon, taking advantage of the peace in Germany, rode into Spain with 200,000 of his best men to take brief control of the Spanish situation, bringing the total French forces in Spain to 330,000 of which 60,000 are cavalry and 400 artillery. His one goal, to launch a lightning attack that would crush Spanish resistance and push the British back into the sea.

The superior armed French forces soon began to come between the scattered British forces before they had time to meet up, increasing the danger that the British forces would be destroyed piecemeal. By the end of November the 2/59th were at Pomferada, 150 miles inland. However, the inhospitable terrain and the ill-equipped army had delayed Baird from meeting up with Moore who realised that he could not hope to defeat such overwhelming odds and on 28 November ordered that all British forces should fall back to the coast in the north and sail for Lisbon.

Spanish officials begged Moore to stand and fight with the backing of Spain's armies, six days later however on 4 December, with the Spanish armies dissolved to nothing, the French Imperial Guard marched into Madrid. Spain had fallen.

Moore refused to retreat without issuing a bloody warning to the French first. Despite being outnumbered 10 to one, Moore, in receipt of some captured French dispatches revealing Marshal Soult's positions and weakened forces, felt confident that he could strike at Soult's position north-west of his armies and inflict some damage. Having met up with Baird on 18 December, Moore had completed the deployment of his troops by 22 December, ironically the same date that Wellesley was cleared of all charges for his part in the Cinta Convention. News reached Moore on 23 December that Soult was coming to do battle and was less than 24 hours away, however another French force was approaching from the south-west that threatened to surround and annihilate Moore's tiny force. Moore was left with no choice but to disengage his troops and order a retreat back into the mountains.

Moore's troops, already disheartened by the fact that they were in full retreat without even losing a battle, now faced a long march back through the inhospitable mountains in the face of a bitter winter. Rivers had already begun to flood and swell and sheets of icy blasts meant that the rear-guard, composed of Craufurd's Division, found great difficulty in holding off the French cavalry that was swarming the entire area trying to break through into the British lines.

Destroying every abandoned village and bridge behind them, Craufurd's division seemed to be the only aspect of the British army that retained it's discipline and cool-headedness. Men of other units were using every pause in the retreat to loot houses and raid stores and cellars for strong drink, as army discipline gradually ebbed away through cold, hunger and desperation.

Those too drunk to march were left as easy prey for cavalry patrols whilst any mutterings from the ranks earned them a few hundred lashes to keep the men in check. The whole retreat had turned into a desperate contest for survival and every yard of ground had to be fought for in a series of rear-guard actions to keep the French at bay. During the 59th's retreat to Lugo they turned and struck a blow for the British at the River Mino. The 59th had been brigaded with the 51st and 76th regiments and were tasked with holding the extreme left of Moore's position. The brigade was attacked by a superior amount of infantry, supported with five cannons but using the narrow passes of the ravine to their advantage they managed to turn back the French attack but at the cost of slowing down the British retreat.

By mid January, the heavy snows had turned to slush with men marching with bloodied feet, empty bellies and disconsolate hearts. Shoes, equipment, dead horses and abandoned carts all littered the routes the British troops marched down. Napoleon quit Spain for

France on 2 January 1809, certain the British were beaten and that Soult could finish the job for him. Between 6 and 8 January, Soult caught up with Moore and prepared to attack. Moore managed to scrape together what few men he had that were battle ready, but neither army had the stomach to fight in the bitter mountain winter and so what little morale the British troops recovered at the prospect of a fight was soon worn away again.

On 11 January the first British troops reached Corruna. The combination of horrendous conditions and sporadic fights between piquets and rear-guard actions had cost the British around 5,000–6,000 men. Those hoping to receive a hearty welcome were sorely disappointed to discover that their troop transports were delayed at Vigo Harbour and now the British had their backs to the sea.

With Moore desperate to hold off the ever enclosing French, British troops that gradually staggered into Corruna, were issued with a hot meal, new shoes and blankets, and ordered straight to the battle lines drawn up by Moore. The 59th amongst this number could only bring 300 men to the field and were dispatched to the left of Moore's line. With positions outside of the town to hold off the advancing French, the first troop transports arrived between 11 and 15 January to take away the sick, wounded, and lame. Lacking any cavalry whatsoever, all of Moore's 15,000 men were infantry excluding his eight British and four Spanish artillery pieces. Despite his troops being weary and worn down, an inexhaustible Moore personally oversaw the positioning of the troops and defences, running between commanders and taking a few minutes to stop and shout words of encouragement to his men.

With the rest of the troop transports arrived, Moore prepared to stand and fight, whilst the wounded, sick, civilians, cavalry and guns were boarded at dawn on 16 January. Around 2pm three guns sounded from the Monte Mero where Moore's weakest flank was. Soult had come to battle.

The French with a similar number of men but more artillery, tried to simultaneously attack Moore's left (Monte Mero), centre, and right. The 2/59th took a strong battering from the French artillery and were brought forward to plug the gap after the 81st regiment had taken such a hammering that they had to be pulled from the line. The 59th's commander Lt. Col. Fane was hit in the head by a musket ball as the 59th fell into line and command fell to Captain Fairfield of the Grenadier Company. Both the Grenadier and Number 1 Companies charged the advancing enemy and scaled a fence under heavy fire causing the French to check their advance. When Captain Wilson of Number 1 Company was wounded Lieutenant Mandeville of the Grenadier Company took command of both companies and directed their charge against the French. In charging the French positions the 59th Grenadier and Number 1 Companies were now the furthest forward in Moore's army and as darkness fell and with both armies weary and not gaining any advantage, the fighting gradually ceased at 8pm with the two 59th companies being the last to disengage from the battle with a total of 60 killed or wounded from their fateful charge.

Exhausted, and with no stomach to pursue, the French allow Hope to retire unmolested to Corruna where the rest of his shattered army embarked. As if the defeat was not disheartening enough for the British, Moore, in his fashion of overseeing the whole operation exposed himself too much to the French artillery and was hit in the breast by a French cannon ball, shattering his ribs and taking off his arm. Command fell to Sir John Hope whilst Moore was carried to Corruna where the beloved commander died shortly after 8pm (just as the hostilities ceased) and was buried at Corruna on 17 January, much to the sorrows of his men.

The rest of the army began to embark on their transports and even then the 59th were not safe from enemy fire when the ship carrying their HQ Staff was hit by a French shore battery and began to sink. The regimental colours were almost left behind until Sgt. Major Perkin ran below deck and retrieved them before they sank with the ship!

By the evening of 17 January the last British transport was sailing out of Corruna on its five-day passage back to England.

All of Northern Spain and the majority of Portugal was back in the hands of the French. However, Craddock, overlooked as a mere inconvenience by the French, still held on to a tiny spit of Southern Portugal with 12,000 men in preparation for a British return, whenever that may come.

The Second Iberian Campaign

Walcheren – Talavera – Busaco – Torres Vedras – Fuentes d'Onoro - Albuerra

With Burrard remaining in England to face an enquiry into the fiasco following the landing of the army in Spain in 1808, Wellesley was acquitted from any blame and ambitiously applied to command the next invasion force. On 7 March Wellesley delivered an official report to the government commenting of the situation in the Iberian Peninsula. Securing their backing, Wellesley was awarded command for the next invasion and managed to secure the allocation of 20,000 troops, of which 4,000 were cavalry. Wellesley was also to be allowed to reorganize the Portuguese army and to encourage and provide the

Spanish with whatever resources necessary that they could use to wage guerrilla warfare against the French.

As Moore's battered army was fighting its way back through Spain to Corruna, rumours began to emerge in Europe that the Austrian and Prussian armies were massing against the French in the east. To counter the threat Napoleon began to mass troops in 1809 in eastern France. After landing back in England the army only had a few months to recruit and train men to replace those lost in the retreat of Spain before they were issued with their next campaign in July 1809.

40,000 troops under the overall command of the Earl of Chatham with Sir Eyre Coote as his deputy and Sir Richard Strachan commanding the naval force of 58 ships were sent to the Scheldt Estuary to occupy the island of Walcheren and capture Antwerp in Holland. The campaign served two purposes. The first was to destroy the enemy fleet already congregated there and prevent Napoleon from massing any further navies there to use as a launch pad to attack Britain and the second was to open up a 'second front' to cause the French to alleviate the pressure growing in the east by causing the troops being massed to fight the Austrians to be dispatched to Holland.

The first troops landed on 11 August and launched their first objective to take the town of Flushing to be able to secure a landing point to disembark the guns and horses. Lt. Col. Fane was placed in command of the disembarkation area and so Major McGregor led the 59th in the besieging of Flushing, which began on 16 August. The siege was not an easy task as in order to bog down the British army the French had opened the sluice gates to the island and flooded the surrounding area. The siege lasted two weeks until the British guns were brought up and bombarded the town, which capitulated two days later.

Despite the fall of Flushing, Chatham was slow to act upon his success and instead of pursuing allowed the troops to stagnate allowing Marshal Bernadotte to bring up 26,000 fresh troops to reinforce the main garrison at Antwerp. The boggy ground and the late summer heat soon bore something much more deadly than enemy fire, the dreaded 'Walchern Fever.' This malaria type fever swept indiscriminately through the British ranks decimating their number. Losing such large numbers in a short time disheartened the expedition and Chatham ordered the abandonment of the campaign in late 1809. Whilst none of the main objectives had been met, the campaign had succeeded in drawing troops off the eastern front to bolster the coastal fortifications and garrisons along the Atlantic. In February 1810 the expedition was called home to England but was in a very bad way. Walcheren had cost the British a total of 15,000 casualties, 4,000 were lost in Holland to the fever, a further

11,000 were incapacitated by its effects, some of this number died on the voyage home. Only 106 men had been lost to enemy action during the campaign. The 59th had lost 66 men to the fever, which was relatively small in comparison to others, who lost up to 75% of their strength, but it wouldn't be until 1812 when the 59th would see enemy action again.

The engagements in both Spain and Walcheren had been a tough lesson for the British army. Due to over confidence, lack of suitable resources and any clear strategy the armies had suffered terrible losses with more men succumbing to diseases, hunger and the elements than to any real enemy action. Now that he had gained full command of the army in Spain, Wellington had a clear strategy in his mind of how to defeat a superior enemy and all the while keeping his troops fed, clothed and in supply of everything needed for an advancing army.

When encamped, Wellington's army was a hub of activity with at least double the amount of civilians milling around than actual troops. Despite the British Army possessing their own Commissariat Department that was responsible for the provision of clothing, food, and ammunition; merchants, hawkers and sutlers (employed tradesmen) were allowed to accompany the army as it marched through selling whatever necessities and luxuries to the men were required. The further from the nearest port or major city the army was, the thinner the supply lines became and the more difficult it became to protect them from enemy attacks and maintain the provisions whilst travelling. Some of the more favourable commodities sold by sutlers and merchants to the troops were local beers and spirits, local food and produce, local brown Portuguese cloth, which after many hard months of campaigning became more prominent on the red jackets than red cloth itself, tobacco and fruit. The 45th made a name for themselves as hardy marchers inspiring William Grattan of the 88th to write about them *'Then there was the first rate battle regiment, the 45th, a parcel on Nottingham weavers, whose sedentary habits would lead you to suppose they could not be prime marchers, but the contrary as the fact...'*

Another common sight in the army were camp followers and wives, often with their families, marching with their soldier husbands and lovers. Once a man enlisted, he was expected to spend every day of his armed forces life in the army barracks for training and parade. Therefore, soldiers who enlisted already with wives were allowed to bring them to live on the barracks with them. However, the women were expected to earn their own keep and to not impede the army whatsoever. Unfortunately, this often meant some tried to earn extra money through prostitution, but those whose actions were thought to bring moral stagnation or any unethical activity of their

Regiment into question could find themselves summarily drummed out and abandoned. Whilst this was practical on home soil, once a regiment went away to foreign fields to fight, it would be impossible for every man to bring his wife with him. Every company therefore, was allotted six wives, drawn by straws, to follow them on campaign, whilst the rest would remain in England. However, the women were expected to share the hardships of their husbands and though camp wives were allowed to draw rations, their daily allowance was half that of the men folk, and this they were expected to provide for any children with as well.

However, once the army had reached foreign lands, it was not uncommon for soldiers to strike up acquaintances with local girls who, seeking an escape from their difficult home lives, quite often followed their new soldier lovers as the army progressed through their country. Whilst the army found that the native girls proved useful in translating and also for their knowledge of local area, some even having connections to the bands of guerrillas, unfounded reports of a rather disturbing event at Bordeaux harbour in 1814 that would suggest that British gratitude was rather limited. Whilst the army had been happy enough to allow Spanish and Portuguese women to accompany them right up until their victory at Toulouse in 1814 bringing about the capitulation of France, they suddenly found themselves with the problem of having a long trail of women, many young girls who had sought British protection, whom they were unable to do anything with. Though some had married their soldier husbands and even had children with them, they were not recognised as valid marriages, merely simple peasant rituals. Many soldiers, who were bound back for England, found themselves being torn from their families who were abandoned on a French harbour with no means of even getting back home to Spain.

Whilst the men were expected to perform their duties in the field, women were similarly expected to carry out certain duties in maintaining the camp. As well as taking care of their own families, women in camp were expected to act as cooks, washer women, and seamstresses, and in an army that was still forty years away from any proper medical services and Florence Nightingale-esque characters to reform the army nursing system, women could also be expected to assist the surgeons in their gruesome tasks.

However, officers who brought their wives abroad with them could expect a very different standard of living. Wives of officers still had their duties to perform, however, rather than washing clothes and mending jackets, their duties merely required them to uphold their social conventions in hosting dinner parties for the officer class and to charm senior officers in the hope that this may gain their husbands a higher commission.

Wellington's army in the Iberian Peninsula had moved on very little from the Cromwellian style army of two hundred and thirty years before. In a society that was still quite feudal and paternalistic, those of the higher classes saw it as their right and duty to guide the lower classes that they deemed to be of lower intelligence and in need of direction.

Whilst most senior regimental officers such as Colonel's and Major's, who may have had many years experience of soldiering, discovered a paternal responsibility to the men under their command, many junior officers such as Captains and Lieutenants were young men straight out of schooling who looked upon the war as a form of entertainment and an adventure. In fact it was the breaking out of hostilities in Europe that put an end to the Grand Tour that most young aristocrats would go on for two or more years once their schooling was complete, to take in arts and culture. In a time before officer training schools, when commissions in the armed forces could be purchased, despite the officers having no experience whatsoever, most rich young men tended to view the war in Spain as an adventure and entertainment that was far removed from their strict home lives. They also tended to bring with them their attitude that the common soldiers were there to be of personal service to them and rather than lead by example, they often relied on the more experienced NCO's to lead the men, but could also be quite condescending and patronizing to the lower classes. Any officer, due to their social standing, was automatically exempt from flogging as a punishment, but risked losing their commission or worst still bringing shame upon their family name if found guilty of an offence. Whilst the officers of the 45th were widely regarded as being brave and well-disciplined one record of the period describes how a Lieutenant William Pearce of the 45th was 'honourably acquitted' of being involved in a drink-fuelled brawl at a brothel. Wellington had urged the Court Martial to re-word their pardon as though the officer was found not guilty his honour and family name was still at stake until he had been honourably acquitted.

Officers, if they paid enough, could take certain privileges abroad with them, on top of their standard army kit. Officers often travelled with three or four valises full of luxury items, horses, servants and side arms such as their own pistols. Standard items could include paintings, books, perfumes, candlesticks, silver plate, writing equipment, sketchbooks and liquor. Comparatively, the common soldier would have to carry his livelihood in his Trotter's knapsack and was allowed only a few luxury items. He was also expected to carry at all times as part of his kit a spare shirt, spare trousers, spare stockings, second pair of shoes and cobblers kit, razor and soap. Small luxuries he may have would be a pewter plate and mug, cutlery, and were he slightly literate and religious perchance a Bible.

Wellington, knowing that the bulk of his army comprised of

men who were not used to respecting authority and were often too fond of the bottle and strong liquor, had to implement methods of discipline that would ensure that his men toed the line and did not indulge in behaviour that may bring the already fragile relationship between the allies in the Iberia crashing down around them.

Wellington, a notorious disciplinarian did not spare the rod when it came to ensuring that his troops toed the line. Whilst in Spain, the French succeeded in turning the population against them through acts of brutality, looting, murder, and rape that resulted in mass Spanish resistance and *guerrilla* warfare being waged that seriously hampered France's progression in the Iberia. Wellington, already mistrusted by many Spanish partisan leaders, could not afford to have the population turn against him through any misdemeanours. Any acts that could be detrimental to Anglo-Spanish relations such as looting, rape, murder, or striking an officer, were punishable by hanging. The fear of hanging and the baying mob was often enough to deter some of these more serious offences but it was not always possible for the army to monitor the crimes being committed. In a society before a recognised police force at home let alone in the armed forces, Wellington came to rely on the presence of the provosts, a select force of men, who under the command of the Provost Marshal were responsible for maintaining of army discipline and also to act as guards in camp prisons for soldiers pending trials and court-martials. The worst crime for a soldier to be punished for was, if caught and returned, desertion to the enemy. Napoleon was renowned for not allowing flogging in his army, as he believed that his men followed him through admiration and not through fear of punishment. Those who tried to desert to the French were firstly flogged and then marched to the scaffold where they would subsequently be hanged. Such a bloody spectacle would make any other man contemplating deserting to the enemy lines think twice.

To deter the lesser crimes of drunkenness, theft and ill discipline, Wellington used the common fear of flogging and to keep his men in order and to maintain army discipline. The number of lashes a man received depended on the severity of his crime. A hundred may be received for a minor offence such as drunkenness or loss of equipment and uniform, but some records show of men being sentenced to over one thousand lashes for serious crimes such as desertion. Desertion was considered an extremely serious offence, particularly as the army was so small that every man counted. Flogging was designed to be prompt, set an example, and to effectively deter any further similar activities.

Flogging, within an infantry battalion, was carried out in public in front of the unfortunate victim's comrades who were formed in a hollow square and supervised by the regimental surgeon, the adjutant and the drum major. Stripped from the waist up with their back exposed and depending on the amount of lashes sentenced, floggings often required a string of drummers to carry out the task once their own strength sapped with the length of punishment. Though one of Wellington's more dependable regiments the 45th still had it's fair share of malingerers who would try avoid duty. In 1813 Thomas Beckwith of the 45th tried to cut the tendons in his foot to make himself unfit to serve. He was sentenced to one thousand lashes but only received 550 when his punishment was halted by the surgeon as he was very close to death.

Every regiment in Wellington's Army would have been distinguishable by two elements that were personal to that Regiment and that Regiment only, these were of course the Regimental March and the Regimental Colours.

Regimental marches were often used to rouse the spirits of the men to remind them of their families back home and what they were fighting for. Drummers, and occasionally buglers, had a different role to play than the rest of the Regimental Musicians. Whilst the musicians followed behind the line into battle, drummers marched in front, beating out a steady march or orders for manoeuvre through the noise and fog of battle when it became almost impossible to see or hear any orders being given.

Often represented as young boys, Regimental drummers could be the son of a serving soldier in the regiment who could help his family earn a few extra pennies by following his father into the ranks from an early age. As well as his drum and sticks, drummer boys also carried in their pack a *cat o'nine tails* for flogging duties. Flogging played an integral part in maintaining the discipline in Wellington's Army. Drummer boys were encouraged to perform their flogging duties to the best of their abilities as this served to give them strong upper bodies for handling muskets and also nerves of steel when in battle.

Musicians and the Regimental band also had an integral part to play in battle as well as on the parade ground. Having played the men off into battle, the musicians would then follow the advancing lines and act a stretcher-bearers, carrying the wounded back to the awaiting surgeons and their instruments.

Like the regimental band, the colours would also have an important part to play serving a variety of roles both on and off the battlefield. Regiments would possess two colours. The first was the King's Colour, 6ft by 6ft 6ins, on a 9 ft pole, the Union Flag with regimental insignia in the middle. The second set of Colours were the Regimental Colours which similar in size to the King's Colour bore the Regimental facing (green for the 45th, white for the 59th) with a small Union flag in the top corner.

Had the Regiment been involved in previous conflicts and battles they may also have their 'Battle Honours' sewn into the cloth to commemorate their historic lineage and also to remind the troops of their previous victories and regimental ancestry.

Regimental colours were often venerated with the same respect as Holy relics, and in order to ensure their safety in battle were charged to the protection of a Colour Party. Colour Parties could range from sixty to twenty men who under the command of an Ensign, the officer in charge of their protection, and the supervision of the Colour-Sergeants, they often attracted most attention from enemy actions.

Whilst on the march, colours were carried at the head of the marching regimental column to give the Staff an idea of which Regiments were present on the march but also to act as morale boosters for flagging and weary troops. In battle the colours could be used as rallying points and makeshift markers, but again, the sight of their colours in battle acted as a strong symbol to the Regiment of what they were fighting for, not only their pride, but their King and families back home.

In as much respect that Colours were held in, it was likewise seen as the ultimate disgrace to lose them or have them captured by the enemy in battle. Regiments that were unfortunate to find themselves in such a situation, were not only subject to the scorn and ridicule of the rest of the army, but also could find themselves being stripped of their honours and made into a Battalion of Detachments, with their men sent to other Regiments and officers forced to sell their commissions.

Like many of the other British Line Battalions, the 45th and 59th were composed of between 600–1,000 men and broken down into ten companies consisting of eight line companies, one Light Company and one Grenadier Company. Light Companies were made up of the lightest and nimblest men of the battalion, who were trained to be excellent marksmen. Light Infantry Companies first came into practice during the American War of Independence from 1776–81, when battalions at the time needed to form an arm that enabled them to combat the American militiamen who would take advantage of the dense woodlands and settlements to conduct partisan activity on the British forces. The British suffered heavy casualties at the hands of these guerrilla movements, and so it was decided that each battalion would train men especially for counter-partisan activity.

The Light Infantry's job was to scout ahead of the battalion on the march, provide rear cover, and when in battle to harass the advancing enemy by taking pot shots at their officers and to attempt to disrupt their lines of communication. The Grenadier Company, on the flip side, was made up of the tallest and strongest men of the battalion. During the Wars of the Spanish and Austrian Successions, the Grenadiers were soldiers trained to throw grenades, small shells with fuses, at the enemy and break their morale. To achieve maximum throwing potential, the men chosen were tall and strong and wore mitre shaped hats so that no part of their uniform got in the way when they threw their projectiles. Though by the time of the Peninsular War, men of the Grenadier Company had found their profession obsolete and instead were more practically used for parade duties as the battalion's smartest and tallest soldiers.

By the time of the Peninsular, both the Light and Grenadier Companies wore the same uniform as their Line Company colleagues but maintained the insignias of their ancestral profession, the Grenadiers, a blazing grenade, the Light Company, a bugle.

Behind the line the battalion's support staff and other ranks could be found. Every battalion had their own party of pioneers who, distinguishable by the axes they carried, were to cut down trees for firewood or defence-works, and to carry out any manual tasks.

On campaign, like at home, the infantryman's day was taken up with drill, training and parade. Whilst life in camp on campaign could prove to be an exciting venture, the period of a soldier's training was long and arduous, with special emphasis placed in marching, standing to attention and firepower. Mostly, the success of the British infantryman relied heavily on his discipline and firepower; his training period consisted of nine weeks of marching, standing, and firing as one body with up to 800 other men.

Image supplied by Kevin Wolf of Deviouswolf Photography©

The line infantryman's 1797 India Pattern 'Brown Bess' musket was perhaps his most precious piece of equipment that would prove to be the only thing that stood between him and death. Capable of firing up to three rounds a minute, the infantryman was trained to load, prime, ram and fire a round averaging every twenty seconds and to maintain a steady rate of fire. In his cartridge pouch he would carry up to sixty balls in greased paper cartridges that made the ball easier to ram down the barrel. The man would firstly bite off the ball and its charge from his cartridge, he would pour the remainder of his powder from the cartridge into the barrel and spit in his bullet. Next he would level his musket and pull back the hammer and pour the powder into the pan and finally he rammed the bullet home using the ramrod. Preparing and firing his musket was no easy feat and made even worse through the drying out of his mouth through saltpetre in the gunpowder, bruising his shoulder through the fierce back-kick of the musket and also the pan would spew out black smoke, sparks and hot wadding from the cartridge every fire. After a few volleys the men would be parched, blinded, deafened, stained and also in pain from not only their bruised shoulders but also their fingernails would be cracked and bleeding from continually having to change the flints. His other form of weaponry to carry at all times was his socket bayonet, 15 inches of cold steel that fitted, albeit rather loosely, on the end of the musket and was held in place by a locking mechanism. The bayonet gave the musket an extra 15 inches of reach and was used most effective in infantry charges or to fend off cavalry attacks. However, when a bayonet was fixed it made firing the musket more difficult and often impeded the men's range of firing, it was at this point that they came to depend on the closeness and steadfastness of their comrades to hold their rank and fight off the enemy with every breath in their body.

Back on the Iberian front, Wellesley was offered the role by the Portuguese government to take supreme command of their armed forces; he declined. Instead he offered the position to his personal friend Sir William Carr Beresford. Wellesley was given the promotion he had been waiting for, overall command of British and allied forces in Portugal, on 6 April 1809 and on 22 April he arrived in Lisbon with one clear objective, the defence of Portugal, bringing with him fresh troops, fresh stores and most importantly an army that now had the political and social backing of the people back home. In the months following Walcheren, Wellesley had already launched a new offensive in Spain. He specifically asked the government not to send him any 'Walcheren regiments' for fear that these regiments were so weakened by the campaign they would be ineffective in battle and risked bringing the fever over to the army in Spain.

Wellesley's return to the Iberian Peninsula was met with joint welcome by the troops who stayed in Portugal and also by the

Image supplied by Kevin Wolf of Deviouswolf Photography©

Portuguese populace. Not one to lose any time, Wellesley already had plans to move against Soult within forty-eight hours in a lightning thrust north. Wellesley divided his forces into divisions, giving each one an inexperienced Portuguese brigade to train on the march and dispersed them to face the multiple threats in the form of Marshal Soult in the north and Marshal Victor in the east. General Mackenzie, with his brigade to which the 45th were attached, was left to face off Marshal Victor whilst Wellesley and 16,000 troops moved north to head off Marshal Soult, the hope being he would destroy one force and quickly return to move against the other before they had chance to link up.

On 8 May Wellesley's forces came upon Soult's superior forces across the River Duoro. Soult, completely surprised by Wellesley's appearance, as he had been expecting an attack from the west towards Oporto, hastily redirected what troops he could to man the banks of the Duoro and ordered that all bridges and crossing points be destroyed, resulting in Wellesley's troops having to cross in civilian barges all the while under a heavy French artillery bombardment. Either through error or feeling over confident Soult did not fortify the Bishop's Seminary, a large, high walled building to the north of the proposed landing area of Wellesley's troops. As the troops emerged from their barges, they found the ground in front of them unmanned and quickly ran to occupy the Seminary. Over 600 British troops were inside the building before Soult realised his mistake. General Foy directed an artillery barrage onto the seminary to try and smoke the British defenders out, but an allied battery silenced his efforts. With the seminary secured the rest of Wellesley's force crossed the Duoro with ease and were soon engaged with an ill-prepared and surprised French force. The battle was lost before it had even begun, as the last British troops crossed the Duoro and leapt from their barges, the French were retreating towards Amarante. Oporto was back in the hands of the allies, and Wellesley had secured his first victory as supreme commander.

With Soult in retreat from Spain, Wellesley now turned his attentions to Marshal Victor in the south who was based at Merida. If facing a superior French force for the second time was not daunting enough for Wellesley, he also had the extra burden of having to rely on his Spanish allies under the overall command of the ailing General Cuesta for their co-operation and experience. Spain had proved so far to be an unreliable ally to the British and had offered very little in response to repulsing the French from the Iberian Peninsula. Their troops were poorly led, ill-disciplined, and lacked any proper equipment or leadership.

However, having seen what Wellesley's army was capable of at the Duoro, the Spanish seemed to find a new respect and enthusiasm in their British allies and in a surprising move, Cuesta offered to feed, clothe, and provide for Wellesley's troops if his 35,000 Spaniards could attach themselves to Wellesley's force for their attack on Victor. With only 20,000 men to his name in face of Victor's 50,000, Wellesley readily accepted these terms. Both armies now proceeded towards Talavera with he 45th, as part of General Mackenzie's Brigade of the 3rd Division advancing at the head of the British army.

On 24 July Wellesley and Cuesta joined forces to the north of the River Tagus. Wellington's new found hopes in his allies were soon altogether squashed when he discovered that the Spanish had not kept any of their promises to provide transport, equipment, food, or any provisions. Trying to make the best of a bad situation Wellington and Cuesta agreed to join forces at Oropessa, about 30 miles from Talavera on 20 July and confront Marshal Victor who was expecting to join up with around 12,00 troops of Joseph Bonaparte's army. On 24 July Victor retreated towards Madrid and Cuesta, defying all orders and infuriating Wellesley, gave chase only to find himself alone and outnumbered resulting in a mauling by the French army. Wellesley refused to budge from his position and help Cuesta, and on the morning of 27 July the British army was drawn up into three main positions facing Victor's forces. On the right, Cuesta and his Spaniards held the right flank; the British occupied the left flank that comprised of the Cero de Medellin, a large and naturally fortified hill that was impossible to climb, and the centre where British troops were formed to take the brunt of the French attack.

The French attacked on 27 July in three columns, the first column was expectedly repulsed on the slopes of the Medellin, the others were broken up by the resoluteness of the British troops but nothing had been achieved by either side, the only major incidents of the day being the near capture of Sir Rowland 'Daddy' Hill by French voltigeurs and a bayonet charge by British troops that sent a French column reeling back.

Around 3pm that day Wellesley and his staff, positioned near the 45th and 88th (Connaught Rangers) were talking to Lt. Col. Guard when out of nowhere a swarm of French voltigeurs appeared sending the 88th into total confusion and almost captured Wellesley and his staff. It was only due to the resilience of the 45th and some companies of the 60th Rifles that the enemy were held off long enough for Wellesley to make his escape.

Around 5am the following morning a single French gun fired, signalling to 60 artillery pieces to open up a mass bombardment on the Medellin which forced the British defenders to retire back beyond the slopes out of the guns range. The French aim was simple, hold down the British defenders with oppressive fire and march a column up the hill under the cover of artillery fire and sweep the British from their positions.

The British skirmish screen and light infantry that held the crest of their ridge found themselves at times bowing in the face of a massed French infantry onslaught and artillery bombardment but fortunately for Wellesley they kept their cool and eventually managed to repulse a massive French column numbering some 4,500 men with superior and well aimed firepower. Again at 1pm another attack was launched in a different part of the British line following a massed artillery bombardment but again the French column was repulsed following a heavy battering by well trained and steady British infantry volley fire. As the columns began to break some battalions found their enthusiasm got the better of them and broke ranks to chase their fleeing enemy down the ridge slopes. Those that did received a mauling as their prey turned on them.

The 45th, along with the 48th and 52nd – numbering around only 3,000 men, bravely stood to face an over bearing force of 15,000 French as they sought to exploit the gap in the line. Only when the French had got within 50 yards of them did they open up a devastating and well-timed volley fire causing panic in the French ranks. Despite the massed ranks pressing on, the battalions fired volley after volley until the enemy were piled thigh high on top of each other, such were the denseness of the French ranks, and it was only when a cavalry charge of Dragoons was made that the French formation eventually broke and scattered leaving some 1,700 casualties behind them. Despite their charge that broke the French advance, another charge by the 23rd Light Dragoons and 1st Light Dragoons of the Kings German Legion, overstretched themselves whilst pursuing the fleeing French and found themselves trapped in a dried up river bed, where many men and horses broke bones in the jump. Those that made it to the other side of the drop found themselves easy prey for awaiting French cavalry.

Around this time the 45th were ordered to split their forces in two. Six companies under the command of Major Gwyn to help plug the allied centre, and four companies under the command of Captain Smith were to cover the retreat of some battalions who broke in the face of the superior French infantry attacks. Smith and his charge suddenly found themselves embroiled in open rank with French cavalry and after a desperate stand they fought off the French troops long enough to extricate themselves to safety.

The battle of Talavera gradually petered out towards the evening of 27 July as the French failed to succeed to break through the British lines. Though the British held on to their positions they were too exhausted to pursue the retreating French and so Victor was able to limp away and lick his wounds.

Overall, Talavera had cost the British 5,365 casualties in comparison to the French 7,268. Within those British casualties, the 45th loss rate stood at 13 rank and file and five officers killed.

Major Gwyn, two lieutenants, one ensign and 130 rank and file were wounded. A Major Lecky, one sergeant, and ten rank and file were rendered missing in action. Perhaps the most detrimental loss to the battalion in its first major action was the wounding and capture of Lt. Col. Guard who was wounded three times during the battle as he pressed his men to repulse the French attackers. In his official dispatch Wellesley wrote of the 45th; *'Upon this occasion the steadfastness and discipline of the 45th regiment were conspicuous...'*

Due to their actions that day in relentlessly holding off superior French offensives and for standing their ground repeatedly in the face of French artillery bombardments, the 45th were awarded the nickname 'The Old Stubborns' and became widely renowned in the army for their bravery. The 45th were not the only battalion to distinguish themselves that day, however. Most of the troops at Talavera had not eaten proper provisions for weeks owing to their Spanish allies inability to feed them, many of them lacked the proper equipment and most lacked basic shoes, blankets, and greatcoats. All had marched over 120 miles in less than seventy-two hours. In spite of their great victory, the British army on the field that day was one that was weary and on the brink of starvation. Such were their lack of provisions that after the battle the 45th (and no doubt men from other regiments) looted the enemy corpses for any clothing, food or equipment that could be of use to them. A group of the 45th managed to liberate some pantaloons from their French adversaries and swap them for their own torn and bedraggled trousers. Upon seeing them Wellesley questioned an aide who those men were in blue trousers only to be told they were actually men of the Nottinghamshire Regiment!

Wellesley too was to receive recognition for the handling of the army that day. In light of defeating a superior French force and for giving the British government a fresh hope in the British forces under his command he was awarded the title of Baron Duoro and Viscount Wellington – a title that would name him as one of England's finest military commanders.

Talavera was considered to be the most bloodiest and fiercest battle fought to date since the first British troops landed at Mondego Bay in 1808. Wellington shocked by the events of the day and the blatant needless butchery commented in a letter to his brother William; *'Never was there such a Murderous Battle!'* Further tragedy struck both sides when the dry weather combined with the heat of the battle caused a massive fire amongst the long grasses that, indiscriminate to friend or foe, spread over the fields of Talavera burning and choking the wounded and the lame.

Talavera was also the first battle of many in which Wellington employed his strategy of using artillery as support weapons for the infantry instead of applying the French method of using mass bombardment supported by massing infantry.

As line battalions, the 45th and 59th were best employed in engaging the French in defensive positions. Wellington, knowing that he had precious few men to openly engage the French in the field, had to exercise his logistical and mathematical genius and maximise every man he had to hand. Firstly, Wellington had to have a sound knowledge of the French intentions in order to stay one step ahead of a superior enemy. Napoleon was a firm believer in the simple yet effective power of the 'column.' Even from the early days of the Revolutionary Army, Napoleon, as an Artillery expert, was quick to recognise the potential in the use of artillery to break an enemy. He would often open up a battle with a mass artillery bombardment on enemy troops from an artillery park and then under the cover of the bombardment would send forth an infantry column – normally consisting of 1,000–2,000 men packed into ranks who would then smash through the weakened and fragile enemy lines.

This tactic worked well against the poorly prepared Italians and Austrians during the early campaigns of Napoleon's Empire building, however, once he came up against the British in the Peninsula, his favoured tactics were outdated and were easily predicted.

The early defeat in the Iberia had been a costly lesson to the British army hierarchy who due to their own military ineptitude and political incompetence had severely turned the odds against themselves. Whilst the army was professionally trained and highly motivated, it was commanded by arrogant and bungling politicians, who allowed personal grievances to get in the way of their military handling. Officers could purchase their seniority and commission rather than train and work their way into position through age and experience, thus many had received no military training whatsoever, severely limiting their effectiveness and knowledge of battle.

However, much of the downfall of the expeditionary force in the Peninsula owes itself to the fact that the British lacked sufficient artillery, in face of an enemy that was quick to recognize the potential of guns, throughout the period of the Peninsula War and again at Waterloo.

The supply of any ordnance equipment fell to the Board of Ordnance, who since 1669, were placed under the control of a Master General of Ordnance rather than the control of the Commander-in-Chief at Horse Guards. The Board was responsible for the hiring of contracted independently owned artillery teams that would be paid to serve in places of conflict. Unfortunately, most of these independent gun crews were undisciplined and poorly trained, often absconding from battle with the guns leaving the other arms unsupported.

It was only in 1715, at the outbreak of the Jacobite Rebellion, that the Royal Artillery became Britain's first permanent and professional ordnance unit of trained artillerists. The result being that ordnance production and operation could now be undertaken by professional, full-time soldiers who could coherently learn the tasks of their trade, but at the price of the Board losing its privilege of being able to dictate its own terms and costs.

This strong-rooted history and independent tradition meant that despite being at the hub of some of the most notorious innovative discoveries of the period, the Board's lack of co-operation made them reluctant to send Wellington substantial equipment, thus forcing him to make the alternative tactical decisions which were to become his military trademark.

When supporting infantry, artillery would carry with them varied ammunition to inflict various amounts of damage pending the position of the enemy. Aside from the standard round shot, used primarily in the battering of fortress walls, artillery teams also came to rely on the effectiveness of the common shell, a hollow metal casing filled with combustible material, that was designed to explode in the air above enemy troops shattering them with shards of hot metal. In 1784 Lt. Gen. Sir Henry Shrapnel began experimenting with placing smaller projectiles, such as musket balls, inside the case so that when it exploded it threw out projectiles onto the heads of the enemy making it difficult to hide behind solid objects. Shrapnel's invention was first issued as regulatory artillery ammunition in 1804, giving birth to what commonly became known as 'The Shrapnel Shell.'

Whilst solid shot and Shrapnel shells were used as long-range projectiles, artillery could also use close-range anti-personnel ammunition to ward of approaching enemies. Canister shot was perhaps the most deadly weapon in the artillerists' arsenal. The same size as a baked-bean tin, canister comprised a light casing filled with 85–100 musket balls that was designed to fan out upon impact with the ground hitting every target in its path.

Quick to realise that canister was perhaps the most deadly of all artillery projectiles, Wellington came to depend heavily on its use in battle. Ordering an experiment at the Royal Laboratory, Woolwich in 1811, to test the effects of canister, it showed that using canister hit on average 41% of its target. 55 balls hit the same target at 200 yards, 36 balls at 400 yards and a mere 6 balls at 600 yards, the same impact of a whole battalion firing volleys at the same distance.

Lacking any sufficient form of the other arms whatsoever; Wellington came to rely more and more on his Line Battalions and their superior firepower to make up the backbone of the army. The opening battles of the Peninsula War, especially at Corruna, were to prove that the success of the British Army depended on the discipline and stolidity of Wellington's Line Regiments.

Vimiero too, the first battle where Wellington would have to combine his meagre arms together to form these new tactics that would become attributed to him in almost every engagement, demonstrated how the Line Battalions had an integral part to play to compensate for the lack of any other arm.

Wellington, who could match Napoleon in neither Infantry nor Artillery, found that by utilising the landscape to his advantage he could even out the odds stacked against him.

Such severe lack of numbers on Wellington's behalf caused him to try and develop new methods and tactics to put him on an even par against a superior enemy. Never possessing enough artillery to form a substantial 'artillery park' from which he could deliver devastating firepower from a massed point as preferred in the French Order of Battle, Wellington took to employing his artillery in a defensive role supporting the other arms, Wellington preferred to deploy his artillery to well-chosen and well-concealed spots of the battlefield where he would lure the enemy into their path and at a critical moment, would open up fire combined with massed infantry fire.

Adye in the *Bombardier and Pocket Gunner* notes how to position the artillery in the same manner in which Wellington was to come to deploy them as:

[The] guns should be placed as much as possible under cover;
this is easily done upon heights, by keeping them so far back
that their muzzles are only to be seen over them… A battery in the

field should not be discovered by the enemy until the very minute

they open fire, they should be masked by troops. A commander

should use natural landscape to flank himself with e.g. between

streams, hills, thickets to prevent himself being flanked… the shot

from artillery should always take an enemy in the direction of its

greatest dimension.

Using these rules, an artillery commander had gained surprise over the enemy, but had also secured himself into a position by which he could not be flanked or lose the guns. Using this method, Wellington was able to devastate French columns that were marching on his infantry lines by peppering their front with condensed, rapid musket

Image supplied by Kevin Wolf of Deviouswolf Photography©

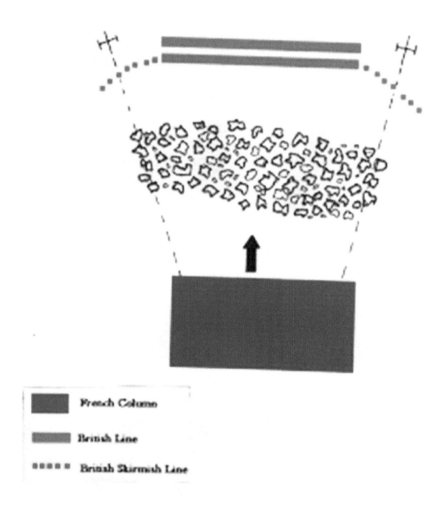

French Column

British Line

British Skirmish Line

fire and battering the column's flanks with artillery cross-fire, thus ensuring that the guns hit a larger target. Writing about the use of this tactic in 1811 Wellington declared:

'I do not desire better sport than to meet one of their columns en masse with our line...'

It was during engagements like these that the 45th and 59th found their mettle tested to the limit and relied on their discipline and firepower that became the making of most line Regiments.

Wellington would have the infantry placed on a hill preferably with a reverse slope. This would serve to (a) screen any movements and (b) would serve to tire out the approaching French column as it progresses up the slope. Ideally the slope would have a very stony approach to it, this would not only cause the column to have to break around solid obstacles, but also mean the British artillery would have an excellent plateau to ricochet their shot off.

The battalion Light Company, also with some elements of the 95th Rifles, would deploy on the crest of the slope screening the rest of the Battalion lining up in formation on the reverse slope.

Image supplied by Kevin Wolf of Deviouswolf Photography ©

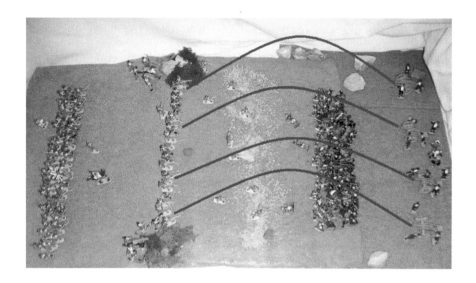

Wellington, would position what few guns he had to support the British line. In order to keep the guns hidden from view until a crucial moment, Wellington would have them positioned further back from the crest, behind hedges or bushes. As the French column marched under the cover of their mass artillery bombardments, the British line at the top would be taking slight casualties from shell and round shot.

From the French first lines of the column they can only see the thin ranks of the battalion's Light Company holding the crest, obscuring their view from any other action, deceiving them into thinking that they could easily smash through.

Once the French reached a certain distance the British guns would then open fire with long-range Shrapnel shell, cleaving holes in the flanks and causing panic in the ranks. However, the dense

ranks meant that the column pushed onwards as men positioned in ranks further back were unable to see the damage being caused in the front.

The battalion's Light Company, and the Riflemen could now start harassing the advancing line. With the battalion ranked in two lines,

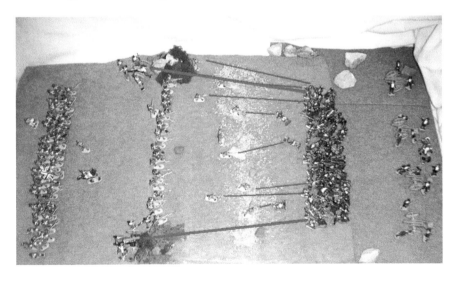

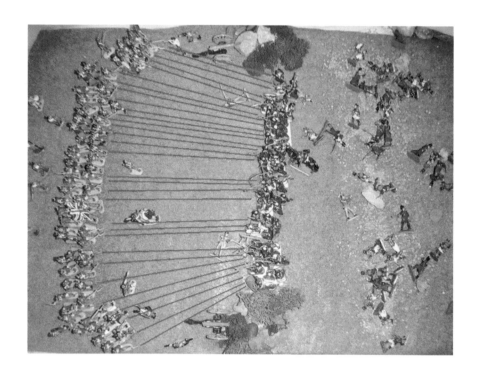

it meant they were able to fire dense volleys into the massed ranks hitting their targets head on every time.

As the column progressed up the hill, their own artillery would have ceased firing for fear of hitting their own men. The front ranks may stop to fire into their British opponents but the massed ranks made it impossible for any man past the third rank of the column to fire his weapon.

Once the French reached the crest of the hill the Light Company retired to the flanks of the waiting infantry just behind the crest. Waiting in ranks of three for the approaching French, the battalion was able to bring to battle all 800–1,000 (pending the size of the battalion) of their muskets and fire devastating volleys into the French ranks. The artillery at this point would now switch to firing canister and cleave massive holes into the flanks of the column. The French were only able to fire around 180 muskets from the first few ranks, but the infantry pressing from the back made it impossible to stop and reload. Facing an enemy with empty barrels and with no time to stop and fix bayonets the front ranks were at the mercy of their opponents. Within minutes, the column would have lost its momentum and begin to falter. Seeing their enemy waver, the battalion now would now fix bayonets and launch a bayonet charge down the hill to break any remaining French morale. Already suffering heavy casualties from a combined artillery and infantry assault, the French would break and flee.

In helping to ensure that this strategy paid off well, Wellington required the full competency of the sergeant's to ensure that the

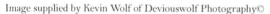

Image supplied by Kevin Wolf of Deviouswolf Photography©

ranks of the British infantry delivered their devastating firepower to maximum impact.

More commonly referred to as NCO's, the role of sergeants and corporals had an incredible impact on maintaining the loyalties of the men in times of hardships and, often acting as mediators between the officers and the men, they frequently had the trust and respect from both parties that otherwise mistrusted each other. Fortunately, the role of NCO was also one that could not be purchased, but was awarded solely on the grounds of bravery or experience. Therefore, most sergeants already had battle honours under their belt, had proved their mettle and had both knowledge and experience that they were happy to share with both officers seeking direction, and men seeking reassurance.

Whilst the officers made their battle arrangements, it was up to the sergeants to offer words of encouragement, admonishment, and support, and mostly to maintain the men in their ranks and ensure they delivered firepower to the best of their capabilities.

Rather than carrying a firearm, sergeants of line battalions carried a *spontoon*. Spontoons, a rather medieval looking weapon, traced their establishment back to the halberd. Aside from a few lancer regiments in the cavalry, most other countries had given up carrying pole-arms in the infantry around the 1750s after the introduction of the socket bayonet had given the infantry the capability of merging the role of pikeman and musketeer into one.

Yet arguably, in a war where gunpowder and musketry established the bulk of the fighting, this very simplistic nine-foot pole with a sharp triangular head and cross bar to prevent over-penetration into an enemy corpse could have ultimately won the war for Great Britain.

Whilst no good as an offensive weapon per say, the spontoon had many uses that were integral to determining whether Wellington's army met with failure or victory.

Firstly, it was effective at maintaining the strong discipline than an outnumbered army heavily needs to ensure they could be trusted in conducting themselves properly. Floggings could be quickly drawn up and received by an A-frame being hastily constructed from three sergeant's spontoons with the perpetrator being tied to them.

As well as their part in enforcing discipline, the spontoon also had its uses in helping to maintain the ranks in battle, which the success of the infantry firepower so depended on. If held horizontally, the spontoon could be used by sergeants to push five or six men together into rank and if need be hold them there to prevent the rear ranks from breaking and fleeing. Finally, sergeants also had an integral part to play in protecting the Colour parties and ensuring that regimental colours did not fall into enemy hands. These Colour Sergeants found their spontoons proved very useful in warding off enemy cavalry that came too close to the Colour party.

Image supplied by Kevin Wolf of Deviouswolf Photography ©

Wellington's army therefore, relied on three major elements to ensure their success when fighting the French; discipline, steadfastness, and pride. Sergeants had a responsibility to ensure all of these criteria were met and despite the spontoon being crude in appearance, it ensured that the job was done.

Because of the resilience of the sergeants and the stolidity of the men, Wellington's application of having infantry and artillery work closely together paid off well and would often result in only around 60 of the 1,000 strong infantry killed or wounded, normally due to the initial artillery bombardment. Of the 2,000 men in the French column, 450–600 men would be wounded, killed and captured.

Despite outnumbering the British in both artillery and infantry, the French battery had only limited firing time, the British guns, however, could maintain a continuous fire for a prolonged period also switching between long range and short-range ammunition.

Whilst the British line infantry were well rehearsed in taking on their French counterparts, fighting cavalry was a different story altogether. Of the three arms that made up the bulk of both armies in the Peninsula, cavalry had an integral part to play, sometimes on the entire outcome of battles. Line battalions were constantly fearful of cavalry attacks as they stood no chance fighting against men on horses who had more manoeuvrability and could seriously disrupt battle formations. Unless protected by a barricade, soldiers stood no chance out in the open unless they could find a way to defend themselves as one body. The standard yet most effective way of defending against a cavalry attack was to form the battalion into 'square' and hold a static position against the cavalry as they swarmed around. Though the square was not a new concept to the

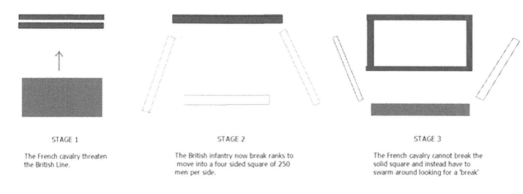

STAGE 1	STAGE 2	STAGE 3
The French cavalry threaten the British Line.	The British infantry now break ranks to move into a four sided square of 250 men per side.	The French cavalry cannot break the solid square and instead have to swarm around looking for a 'break'

Image supplied by Kevin Wolf of Deviouswolf Photography ©

army during the Napoleonic Wars, it was used widely and was a difficult manoeuvre to pull off. Waterloo, the final encounter, bore witness to the effectiveness of forming square but also the dramatic consequences what happens when cavalry caught infantry out in the open.

However, should a battalion be too slow in forming, or as witnessed twice at Waterloo when the Prince of Orange ordered his regiments to advance in a line against cavalry, the cavalry swept round the ranks engulfing the infantry in a melee of sword and death.

Once the order to form square was issued, the battalion, would form a literal square with 250 men on each side, formed three ranks deep.

The first rank would kneel, with bayonets fixed and form a spiked 'hedge' that could be used to ward off approaching horses or to attack the exposed underside of cavalry if they got too close. The second rank would stand firing at the horses, trying to inflict as much damage by firepower as possible. The third rank, pending the threat, could either add to the firepower or fix bayonets and prod out at cavalry and strengthen the hedge.

The staff, drummers, musicians, and Colours would all take position at the centre of the square as a rallying point.

Sometimes, if the enemy sprung a trap or ambush, infantry had very little time to form into a square. William Brown left an excellent account in his memoirs of such an occasion at Salamanca when the 45th were caught out in the open;

As our brigade was marching up to attack a strongly posted column of infantry, a furious charge was made by a body of cavalry upon our Regiment, and, not having time to form square, we suffered severely. Several times the enemy rode through us, cutting down with their sabres all that opposed them. Our ranks were broken and thrown into the utmost confusion. Repeatedly our men attempted to reform, but all in vain – they were as often cut down and trampled upon by their antagonists. At length, however, the enemy was driven off by some squadrons of our cavalry, who came up in time to save us from being totally destroyed. Numerous and severe were the wounds received on this occasion. Several had their arms dashed from their shoulders, and I saw more then one with their heads completely cloven. Among the rest I received a wound, but comparatively slight, although well aimed. Coming in contact with one of the enemy he brandished his sword over me, and standing in his stirrup irons, prepared to strike; but, pricking his horse with my bayonet, it reared and pranced, when the sword fell, the point striking my forehead. He was, however, immediately brought down, falling with a groan to rise no more.'

In such an instance it became a case of every man for himself, and confusion ensued. Some could choose to stand and fight and form groups of men who could stand back to back in closed formation pricking at horses and firing at riders until eventually they too were overrun by sheer enemy numbers or the lucky ones deterred any enemy attacks. If close to natural obstacles such as the edge of a wood or undergrowth, the infantry could try to run towards

Image supplied by Kevin Wolf of Devious Wolf Photography©

and seek shelter from the assault. Most, like Brown, would find themselves having to make snap decisions to stand and fight or flee. If they chose the latter, within minutes they would be chased down by the cavalry and slaughtered, if they chose to fight, they may have at least bought themselves some time although their chances of survival were not too hopeful, but armed with a bayonet they could at least prick at the horses until they fought their way to safety.

After Talavera the British army, weak and weary from battle and lack of provisions, cautiously retreated back into Portugal in a bid to re-strengthen themselves and to await reinforcements. The 45th, now a celebrated veteran regiment, marched back with the British army under Wellington to Badajoz, to prevent the French from invading Portugal from the south whilst Beresford's Portuguese force was covering Cuidad Rodrigo to prevent a northern invasion. The months leading up to Talavera and afterwards had been harsh to the British army and Wellington was desperate for fresh reinforcements. It was during this quiet period that Captain Drew of the 45th was sent back to England in charge of 76 men who had been invalided out of the army. Whilst passing through Leicester the story of the 45th at Talavera had greatly inspired the people of the town who all dug deep into their pockets and generously raised three shillings and sixpence for every man of the party. Captain Drew, an honest and just man, kindly pointed out that only 49 of these men had fought at Talavera, the rest were invalided out due to other actions or through sickness and fever, and after distributing the money for those who fought at Talavera, he presented the remaining money to the Female Hospital of the town.

Whilst Wellington rested his forces on the Portuguese border, his Spanish allies under General Cuesta were growing ever restless to pursue the French still occupying the areas around Madrid. Despite Wellington's warnings however, the Spanish, under the new command of Carlos Areizaga (following a stroke that crippled Cuesta out of the war in August 1809) marched on the French at Ocana but were summarily destroyed on 19 November with a loss of 18,000 men. Ten days later, a Spanish army under the Duke del Parque was utterly annihilated at Alba de Tormes costing the Spanish 40,000 men, 45 guns, and the whole of its baggage train. These two shattering defeats had now completely swept away all of Spain's regular forces, and now guerrilla warfare in the mountains was the only remaining acts of rebellion against the occupying French.

With his Spanish allies now wiped out, Wellington knew the situation was as desperate as ever, to prevent the superior French forces from sweeping over the mountains and sending the British army packing. He knew that in order to defeat the French forces he would have to lure them away from Seville and back towards the Portuguese/Spanish border, forcing them to stretch their supply lines. Between Talavera and September 1810, the British and French now fought a game of cat and mouse with strategically placed British retreats gradually luring the French further and further away from their depots. Wellington's greatest fear was that he would be given cause to engage the French before he had time to fully recuperate his forces. He also had to think about his supply base at Lisbon and ensure he was not cut off from his supplies. There were several major routes the French could take to invade Portugal and Wellington needed to ensure that when they did, it would be at a place he could easily defend. Luring Massena further out he decided to create a false stand at the River Coa and here distributed his forces to prevent any French surprise attack. Though Seville and Madrid were in French hands the British held onto Cadiz, demonstrating that they were far from defeated. In May 1810, Marshal Andrè Massena was given command of 138,000 men with the sole objective of driving the British into the sea. Slowly, the few remaining Spanish held garrisons succumbed to the now seemingly unstoppable French forces and the guerrilla war became extremely bitter with atrocities committed on both sides in acts of revenge.

It was also in early 1810 that Wellington took the opportunity to restructure his army into five divisions. Much of Wellington's army in the Peninsular, especially in the Pyrenean Mountains, had to march in long columns that could stretch several miles. If suddenly needing to engage the enemy, Wellington needed to have all arms ready and could not afford to have his army bogged down as they came into battle. To achieve this, Wellington opted to break down what troops he had at his disposal into brigades and divisions under the sub-command of a Lieutenant General. This meant that Wellington effectively had small pockets of troops consisting of all arms placed all over the terrain making up small armies to deploy quickly in battle, until support divisions came to assistance.

The 45th found itself brigaded with the 88th (Connaught Rangers) and 74th (Highland) Regiments in the reorganization making up part of the 3rd Division that was now commanded by Sir Thomas Picton following the death of Mackenzie. Picton, the son of a Welsh country gentleman, was one of Wellington's more capable Divisional commanders in the Iberian Peninsula. Picton was mostly renowned for his foul language and aggressive mannerism. He often chose to wear civilian dress in battle rather than a uniform, much to the annoyance of Wellington, and often carried a cane or umbrella that he used to personally 'encourage' his men forward into battle with. Never one to let heirs and graces get in the way of gentlemanly conduct, Picton was seen in the aftermath of Cuidad Rodrigo beating drunken soldiers about the head with an umbrella and at Salamanca he leapt from his bed at the sound of the French guns, threw on his nearest civilian coat, and marched out at the head of his division, still wearing his red night cap.

Despite his often odd and aggressive manner, his men thought him a king and sincere gentleman. One sergeant of the 45th once wrote to say that;

'He was strict sometimes, especially about plunder, always talking about how it was wrong to plunder the poor people because countries happened to be at war. He used to flog the men when they were found out; but where he flogged, many generals took life. Besides this, the men thought that he had their welfare at heart. Every soldier in the division knew that if he had anything to complain of, "Old Picton" would listen to his story, and set him right if he could. On the whole, our fellows always thought him a kind general, in spite of his strong language.'

It was during these intricate and arduous manoeuvres between the autumn of 1809 and summer 1810 that Wellington began to lose much of the faith of the British government who, after all of the excitement and enthusiasm following Talavera, had now grown tired of the stalemate between both the forces and begun to question Wellington's command of the army in Spain and also whether the British needed to be there at all.

However, these twelve months of stagnant fighting and minor skirmishes between British rear-guard and French vanguard had not been in vain. With Massena manoeuvred to where Wellington wanted him, he turned to face him on the ridge of Busaco on 26 September.

Despite being able to choose his ground, Wellington was still vastly outnumbered by Massena's 66,000 men and 114 guns to his own 50,000 men and 60 guns. This number would have been made much larger but most of Massena's initial 138,000 force now occupied garrisons strung out across Spain as one by one they fell to his advance.

In a tactic similar to that seen at Talavera and Vimiero, Wellington screened the ridge with infantry and skirmish screens with the main body positioned just behind the crest. The ridge was far too impractical for any opposing force to take and was too littered with natural debris for any column to remain intact whilst marching up. Wellington divided his forces again into three sections mirroring that of Talavera. The Light Division holding the left of the British line, the Portuguese holding the right at the River Mondego under Hill, and bulking up the centre was Wellington's divisions under Picton, Leith and Spencer. Wellington, knew that the element of surprise was important to his success and on the evening of 26 September did not allow his troops to light campfires for fear of giving away his position to the French who were encamped close by.

The morning of 27 September was shrouded by a thick fog that hung in the valley below the ridge where the French were encamped. Around 5:30am the French were pushing against the 5th and 83rd Regiments at the centre of the British line. After being checked by their opposing fire the French turned to their right to exploit the gap between Picton and

Spencer's divisions, this time meeting four companies of the 45th under Major Gwyn and the 88th under Colonel Alexander Wallace, who had raced to the gap and held them off with volley fire, and, seeing their enemy falter, let out a big cheer and followed through with a bayonet charge sweeping them back down the hill.

As another French column attacked the 3rd Division a while later, the light companies of the 88th and 74th began to falter under the pressure of the advance. Seeing their situation, Major Smith of the 45th rode out and steadied the troops who turned and charged their French opponents forcing them to flee down the hillside, a gallant act that saved the position but cost Major Smith his life.

At 6:45am the fog began to lift opening the French positions up to British artillery fire from the left. The persistent French attacks were simultaneously taking place all along the ridge, probing in different areas hoping to find a weakness in the British lines. They almost found a break in the 45th when five companies found themselves enveloped and were forced to retire along with three Portuguese battalions, only being saved by men of Leith's 5th Division who came forward to plug the hole in the line caused by the broken 45th. At 8:30am, a massive French attack was launched by Marshal Ney who sent two columns to sweep away the British who were stationed on the floor of the valley and in less defended areas on the slopes. This massive attack swept the

Portuguese defenders from the village of Sula and also forced the British gunners to abandon their pieces as they swamped the valley floor and pushed up the slopes to reach the crest of the ridge and engaged the skirmish screens of light infantry. As the skirmish screens broke, the ground seemed to spew British infantry and two battalions of British infantry sprang up out of nowhere. Taken completely by surprise, and before they could react, the French found themselves surrounded by Craufurd's Light Division who were firing volley after volley into the flanks of the columns and were so close that they were cutting and stabbing until the column began to break in disarray.

In a battle that closely mirrored Talavera, Busaco had alleviated the British and Portuguese troops of the frustration built up over the previous twelve months, but more importantly the victory gave the British government restored faith in Wellington and the army in Spain. It had also come at a great cost of 1,252 allied casualties and 4,600 French. Of the British casualties the 45th had lost Major Smith, one captain, one lieutenant, one sergeant and twenty-one rank and file killed. Wounded were Major Gwyn, three lieutenants, three sergeants and 106 rank and file. Despite achieving a major victory, the 45th had taken a 42% casualty rate.

The actions of the 45th were recognised by both their divisional commander and Wellington that day. In his dispatch to Wellington, Picton wrote;

'Your lordship was pleased to mention me as directing the gallant charge of the 45th and 88th regiments, but I can claim no merit in the executive part of the brilliant exploit which your lordship has so highly and so justly extolled. Lt. Col. Wallace and Major Gwyn, who commanded the four companies of the 45th emerged on the occasion, are entitled to the whole merit; I am not disposed to deprive them of any part.'

Similarly, Wellington wrote in his dispatches; *'I have never witnessed a more gallant attack than that made by the 88th, 45th and 8th Portuguese regiments…'*

With a harsh winter expected and lacking equipment, provisions, transport and troops to launch another campaign, Wellington now pulled his troops south into Portugal, behind the newly constructed lines of Torres Vedras, a string of fortifications and forts, where he hoped to plan his next move.

In their retreat to the safety of the lines of Torres Vedras, Wellington's army destroyed every grain store, bridge, and warehouse to deprive Marshal Massena's pursuing forces of every comfort. As anticipated, the winter of 1810–11 was a harsh one and Wellington needed to somehow tire out his pursuing foe. Torres Vedras stretched twenty-six miles and covered every possible route to Lisbon. The lines were created by thousands of Portuguese labourers and were manned by 25,000 Portuguese militiamen, 8,000 Spanish and 2,500 British marines and artillerymen. Behind the lines Wellington's army had enough provisions to last out the winter in comparative comfort, whilst in front of them Massena's forces starved on the scorched plains of Portugal.

The cold and bitter winter took its toll on the French who by February were losing 500 of Massena's 50,000 strong force per week, owing to starvation, cold, and disease. In March 1811, Massena gave up his siege of Torres Vedras and slowly began to file his 46,000 men back into Spain. Though Wellington's army was safe, he still did not have the resources to break out and attack Massena. Worse news still was that Soult's forces had defeated a Spanish force and had succeeded in capturing the border fortress of Badajoz.

Following the fall of Badajoz, Wellington broke out from the lines in March 1811 and began to pursue Massena's army. Massena, eager to speed his retreat up ordered that all lame animals be butchered, carts and wagons be abandoned, and unnecessary baggage be left behind. The Portuguese landscape soon became littered with disabled carts, butchered carcases, dead soldiers too weak to keep up, and worse still, razed and looted villages that got caught up in the French retreat. Wellington caught up with Massena at Pombal on 9 March where the 45th, part of the 3rd Division, along with the 5th and Cavalry divisions were concentrated in preparation to attack the French. After a brief skirmish in which one lieutenant of the 45th was killed, Massena continued his retreat along the Mondego.

By 5 April almost all of Portugal was free from the French occupation but Massena had reversed the tables on Wellington in tactical manoeuvres as Wellington had done to him in the build up to Busaco. The pursuing British continued to engage the French in minor skirmishes until they eventually descended out of the Portuguese hills and linked up with the 3rd and 5th Division's awaiting them on the Coa. However, Massena had managed to position Wellington so that he had no option to engage him with 32,00 infantry, 1,200 cavalry and 42 guns in comparison to Massena's 40,000 infantry, 5,000 cavalry and 36 guns at the village of Fuentes d'Onoro.

Fronting the British forces were the 5th, 6th and Light Divisions, with the 3rd Division positioned just behind the village to prevent a French assault from sweeping behind and attacking the flank. Loisson, in a hasty attack tried just this but was held off by a stolid defence by the 3rd Division. During 3 May and 5 May, the 45th and 3rd Division were three times involved in seeing off the French attacks in which time the French took the village twice and both times were beaten back. The fighting in the narrow village streets was bloody with close quarter combat being the only effective way of fighting, with mostly the 88th and 74th being routed from their positions then retaking them in bloody bayonet charges.

In a last ditch attempt the French launched a cavalry attack to sweep the defenders from the village. The 45th completely unprepared for such an attack were caught by the cavalry before they had time to form square and were forced to encounter the cavalry whilst still in line. Such was their determination to hold their position they were able to hold off the cavalry charge and saved the village. Lt. Col. Colin Campbell mentioned this brave stand in his dispatches;

'Lord Wellington, I have reason to believe, ordered the 45th regt, such was his opinion of their firmness, at the battle of Fuentes d'Onoro, to receive in line, and without forming square, the enemy cavalry then advancing in force towards them, if they shall venture to charge. The experiment was not, however made, for the French, I conclude, observing such a steady, determined front presented to them thought it wiser to retire.'

Despite seeing off countless French attacks, the 45th were not heavily engaged at Fuentes and only suffered six losses. Elsewhere the fighting had been bitter close combat, with overall losses totalling 1,545 allies to the French 2,192, with neither side gaining an overall advantage.

Following his defeat at Fuentes d'Onoro, Massena began to fall back upon Cuidad Rodrigo where he planned to replenish his army and meet reinforcements, then attempt to swing north and attack Portugal. Wellington, eager to prevent Massena from linking up with other

French forces split his army in two and sent the 3rd and 7th Divisions north to Badajoz to cover the main northern routes back into Portugal and report any movement by the French. Due to their absence this meant that the 45th missed one of the bloodiest battles of the Peninsular War on 16 May when Beresford's 20,300 British, Portuguese and Spanish contingent came up against Marshal Soult's superior forces at Albuerra. Albuerra is best remembered for its infamous cavalry charges in which the Polish Lancers completely decimated Colborne's brigade after it was caught in line causing some 1,300 casualties of the 1,600 men who comprised the brigade. It also saw frail British lines hold their ground and decimate powerful French columns with relentless volley fire; in turn the French artillery cleaved massive holes in the British ranks with close range fire. Albuerra, although a British victory, had cost Beresford some 6,000 dead and wounded, the French some 7,000. As the armies battered themselves to a standstill, the ground was thick with the bodies of some 13,000 men, a number that would only be surpassed on the field of Waterloo some four years later.

Before the end of 1811 the British forces would launch an unsuccessful siege of Badajoz, and do battle with the French at Arroyo dos Molinos and Tarifa, but nothing would compare to the sieges that would be best remembered in British military history that were to follow in early 1812, Cuidad Rodrigo and Badajoz.

Two Great Sieges:

Cuidad Rodrigo and Badajoz

In January and April 1812, the 45th took part in two of the bloodiest conflicts of the war in Spain when they assisted Wellington besieging and storming the medieval fortresses of Cuidad Rodrigo and Badajoz close to the Spanish-Portuguese border.

With his army poised to invade Spain from Portugal in early 1812, Wellington planned to take the fortresses and pour his army into Spain from between them whilst able to use them as supply bases for a major offensive. Having unsuccessfully taken the fortresses in 1811, Wellington this time knew he must muster a large force behind him and assemble a larger artillery and siege train to batter the walls into submission.

In order to conduct a siege successfully, Wellington required a steady siege train and expert engineers in which he could monitor and launch carefully planned assaults on the city walls, of which he had none. Instead, Wellington's siege artillery consisted of antique Spanish artillery pieces, some of which were reported to have been old Spanish naval guns that had been used against the British during the Spanish Amada of 1588, and a handful of artificers and engineering offices responsible for overseeing the entire planning, whilst the bulk of his infantry was seconded to digging in the siege trenches around the fortress.

Towns would often be besieged from a line of trenches where the artillery pieces, generally 18 pounders were stationed at a range where they could batter at the walls without coming under enemy counter fire. Once the initial trenches were dug the besieging forces would then dig saps towards forward positions and gradually creep towards the enemy walls under cover.

Initially the trenches were dug out of the enemy artillery range and gradually sapped forward in smaller trenches that would begin to link up to form a new line of trenches closer to the fortress. Gradually new batteries were formed where howitzers were employed to 'lob' missiles and incendiaries over the fortress walls at close range to harass the defending troops. At their closest point the trenches were used to mine under the fortress walls where a section would be mined to bring the walls down.

In order to form a breach that was deemed practicable, the engineers would survey a section of the wall that was weakest then order a continuous bombardment of siege artillery fire against the position. The tactics adopted by siege batteries were relatively simple, round shot was fired at two vertical lines on a section of the fortress wall and then fired horizontally in a line between the two vertical lines which hoped to weaken the area literally between the lines. The guns then all concentrated their fire on this area and eventually tried to bring down the section of wall forming it into a 'breach.' This was no easy process though and siege artillery also used up the supplies of powder and shot at an alarming rate, not to mention putting the patience and nerve of the men to the test. Lt. Col. John Jones RE, an Engineer officer present in the Peninsula concluded that to take a garrison of 5,000 men, the besieging army required around 11,000 men to guard the trenches over a period of three shifts, 8,000 men to construct the trenches over four shifts per day and 7,700 supporting services totalling to around 26,950 men.

Once a breach was deemed *'practicable', and enough wall brought down to push an army through, the army was formed up and prepared to throw themselves at the fortress walls in many a futile attempt to somehow dislodge the enemy from their positions.

In preparing for an expected enemy attack, the fortress defenders would have thrown up every kind of obstacle to harass and obstruct the besieging army. Favourite tactics to impede them were to place mines in the fallen masonry and onto the slopes of the breach to surprise the enemy as they approached the summit. Another favoured tactic was to strategically place *cheveaux des frisse,* blocks of wood with sword blades sticking out to snag and obstruct enemy infantry and also to funnel the attacking troops into defending artillery fire from the defences.

As with any battle, there always has to be someone somewhere that takes the opening heat of the battle. The first troops who were to face enemy fire were known as the Forlorn Hope, a unit comprised of two volunteers from each battalion, to be the first to attack the breach. Their job was to be the first to attack the walls and to test enemy firepower. Forlorn Hopes were not expected to survive but any man who did could expect promotion in the ranks. Normally led by Ensigns or Second Lieutenants with bigger ambitions than actual prospects, the success of the Forlorn Hope normally determined the morale of the rest of the waiting army who would be first hand witnessing the horrors unleashed.

For any besieging army launching an assault on a fortress wall, ladders played an integral role in ensuring their success in overcoming the obstacles. Ladders ranged in height from 20ft to 60ft and were carried by the men to the fortress walls where they were then scaled in the face of enemy fire with the men only able to climb one at a time and unable to fire from the rungs onto enemy positions.

Though Wellington's men were sent to take a number of fortresses during the Peninsula War, many such as Burgos, Almeida and San Sebastian fell without too much bloodshed and very little resistance, as they became surrounded by the troops and were basically besieged into submission. However, the storming of the walls of Cuidad Rodrigo and Badajoz in 1812 proved to stretch Wellington's resources to the maximum and though both ended in British victory, they came at a costly price.

The 45th, present at both Cuidad Rodrigo and Badajoz, witnessed the horrors that months of a long drawn out siege could have on battle weary troops. Cuidad Rodrigo particularly, took place on the night of 19 January 1812 after many months of troops laying siege in the bitter winter weather, the infantry who were expected to assault the walls had already spent months having to dig the siege lines themselves without adequate clothing or provisions.

Cuidad Rodrigo was breached in two places after months of heavy artillery bombardment. The first of these breaches was in its northern most corner, which became known as the Main Breach. The second of these breaches was made in the Eastern wall and became known as the Lesser Breach. Wellington's aim on the night of 19 January was to divide his forces and draw off troops from the Main Breach by assaulting the Lesser Breach. Surrounding the walls of Cuidad Rodrigo was a deep ditch which first had to be negotiated and filled to not jeopardize the length of the ladders by the storming party The 45th as part of the first wave, followed a party of 150 sappers who each carried two bags of hay which were to be flung into the ditch from the first parallel to afford a soft landing for the troops following close behind who were to storm the walls. The 45th and another four battalions as part of Picton's 3rd Division, McKinnon's Brigade, found themselves in a ditch too deep and desperately began to flounder over the hay bags towards the breach taking heavy casualties from French cross fire and also from missiles being thrown from the walls. Upon reaching the breach as a disorganized mass, bereft of all order, they swarmed over the slope but were checked by a 16ft drop the other side fronted by trenches packed with French infantry and behind them parapets mounting 24 pounder guns, which caused mass devastation upon the swarming infantry as they reached the lip of the breach. In this area the French also detonated a large mine that killed General McKinnon and caused mass panic. Elsewhere the British were suffering more losses to their command chain as Brigadier-General Robert 'Black Bob' Craufurd, the Irishman notorious for his strict discipline, was hit in the arm and killed, leading his beloved Light Division against the Main Breach, he was to be buried where he fell.

The breakthrough came when the Lesser Breach fell to five companies of riflemen who were able to string out along the walls and fire well aimed shots into the enemy ranks causing panic and providing cover fire for the rest of the Light Division to pour in through the gap and charge the French positions. By this time the French had had enough and had started to retreat from the vengeful British soldiers. Cuidad Rodrigo had fallen.

Once inside the walls, the British soldiers, blood drunk and hell bent on relieving their stress went on a rampage of looting and drinking that caught Wellington and his Staff completely off guard and it took until next morning, 20 January to restore order and have men back to their regiments. Private William Brown of the 45th took part in the assault and recorded that;

'No sooner was the enemy disarmed than all seemed intent on having something for their trouble. The houses, which were in general shut up, were soon broken open, to the ruin of the terrified inhabitants, who stood aghast while they saw their houses pillaged, and their property carried away by their friends and allies, the generous British. Some, more outrageous than the rest, proceeded to even greater extremities; by insulting the men, and subjecting the wretched females to that, which to mention, would make humanity shudder, and wound the delicate ear of virtue. All order and subordination for the time being lost, I spent the early part of the night in

rambling the streets, which were crowded by our men, many of whom were deeply intoxicated, and seemed as happy as if they had all been created dukes of the place. Others, again, more provident, or perhaps more covetous and rapacious, groaned under loads of spoil, which, to any but themselves appeared in vain, as they were not able to carry them off.'

Though Cuidad Rodrigo was a costly affair to the British command structure causing Wellington to lose some able commanders, in comparison to the next siege of Badajoz, it was won with relative ease.

After the fall of Cuidad Rodrigo in January, Wellington turned his attentions to the much larger medieval fortress of Badajoz to his south, which ran parallel to the River Guardiana. Ideally, Wellington hoped that with the winter of 1811–12 behind him, taking Badajoz would be relatively simple in more favourable weather. Though this was more favourable, his previous action at Cuidad Rodrigo had cost him some valuable brigade and division commanders which he did not have time to replace, there was also the issue of still not possessing a proper siege train.

Badajoz, was besieged from the east with its back to the River Guardiana. On 17 March the first parallel was begun by the little improved force of some 120 engineers, sappers and artificers in total, yet once again much of the heavy digging needed to be done by the infantry. By 24 March all six batteries had been dug and positioned, with even ten 18 pounder siege guns arriving from England courtesy of the Royal Navy that were strategically placed amongst the batteries. On the morning of 25 March, with all batteries in place the guns opened up a constant and steady fire that would last until 5 April. Their targets? Batteries four and five were to direct fire upon the south facing wall of Trinidad, batteries one, two and three to direct fire upon the Picurina and battery six to concentrate upon San Roque. Wellington's strategy was simple, open up three breaches and spread the defences as thinly as possible. On 26 March it was ordered that new batteries should be opened up after the fall of the Fort Picurina. Battery numbers seven, eight and nine were formed to bombard the Trinidad and Santa Maria bastions in a bid to breach their walls. By 29 March battery numbers 10 and 11 were formed to begin their bombardment of San Roque. Wellington had hoped to assault the breaches on the night of 5 of April, but with only two breaches made, one at Santa Maria and the other in the Trinidad, Wellington ordered another day of bombardments and succeeded in opening up another hastily made breach just to the west of the Trinidad.

On the evening of 6 April Wellington's forces were drawn up in order of battle. The 4th Division were to attack the San Trinidad, the Light Division were to assault the breach at Santa Maria and Picton's 3rd Division, to which the 45th were a part of, were to assault the Castle to the rear of the fortress. In fact, the assault on the castle was only expected to be a diversionary tactic to draw the defenders away from the breaches at Santa Maria and Trinidad where the main assault was to take place and allow the 4th and 5th Divisions to break in and rush the garrison. However, resistance at the main breaches was much heavier than expected and soon the walls in front of the breaches were filled with dead, dying and wounded British as wave after wave of men were cut down by concentrated musketry fire from the walls and within them artillery bastions firing down onto the disorganized men. Picton received hastily written orders that the attacked on the breaches was failing and that his men must now try to take the castle. The job of taking the castle fell to Major General James Kempt's brigade of the 45th, 74th and 88th regiments.

With only ladders and stolid determination the men at the castle walls rushed up the rungs to try and find a gap in the defences. Unfortunately in the rush both Kempt and Picton were wounded leaving their attack temporarily leaderless. For the men on the ladders, they were being pushed on by their comrades' bayonets from below and were being held off by the enemy bayonets from above. In a small segment of the castle walls, the 45th were heavily embroiled with an embrasure manned by a French unit that were drawn up under the command of an officer ready to meet their attackers. Private William Brown of the 45th took part in the brutal scramble for the embrasure; he later recalled in his memoires that awful scramble to find a section of unmanned wall. He recalled that:

'... a Grenadier officer of our regiment preceded us, who, when his head was nearly on a line with the enemy's feet, was fired at by the officer in front. Missing the contents of the pistol, he instantly gave his opponent a back slap across the legs with his sabre, which fell him over into the ditch. Our officer then leapt onto the embrasure, cutting down all that opposed him, and was immediately followed by the men, who became directly masters of the ramparts...'

That famed officer was Lieutenant William MacPherson of the 45th's Grenadier Company. According to the accounts of Robert Jones, also of the 45th, MacPherson leading his men, found that his ladder was about three feet too short and was physically hoisted by his men to get him to the level of the embrasure where, unprepared for what was at the top, MacPherson was hit by a musket shot in the chest that ricocheted off some Spanish dollars in his breast pocket.

McPherson was thrown from his ladder, which toppled sideways and hit a buttress causing him to fall off and fall beneath. With two ribs broken by the shot and struggling to breathe, MacPherson pressed on back up the ladder but the exertion forced him to retire back to the ditch.

In any case, MacPherson had forced an opening in the enemy ranks and elements of the 45th, 74th and 88th began to pour in and take the ramparts from the defenders.

Undaunted by his wounds, MacPherson now attempted to make his way to the tower where, high upon a flagpole, the French colours were still flying. Fighting his way through the confusion and picking up whatever men he could on the way, MacPherson made his way up the steps to the tower where he found the colours still flying and only one sentry guarding them.

Forcing the sentry to surrender, MacPherson then tore down the colours but finding he had no flag to fly up the pole he stripped off his uniform jacket and hauled it up, symbolising to the watching Staff that the castle had fallen and British soldiers were inside Badajoz.

Sadly, MacPherson's single act of bravery, which could have indeed been recorded as the one of the more famed events to take place that night, has in time become superseded by the more darker events that were to follow. In similar circumstances to Cuidad Rodrigo, the frustrating build up to the siege and the blood lust of the attack had caused the British soldiers, once inside the walls to set course for a three day rampage of drunkenness, looting, murder and rape. Enemy soldiers were hunted out and butchered in the streets whilst houses were broken into and looted for whatever was not nailed down. Women were cruelly treated and any men folk who tried to defend their families from the marauding British troops found themselves beaten or worse. Brown, whose stomach had curdled at the sight of the rampaging troops in Cuidad Rodrigo now bore witness to an even worse sight. He recalled one instance where;

'Looking round the place I perceived a man, apparently naked, walking to and fro in one of the buildings in front of me. Prompted by curiosity I stepped towards him, and having asked how he became reduced to the state he was in, he informed me that being master of the house he had endeavoured to repel the lawless aggressions of my comrades, but being unable to withstand such numbers, they had stripped and turned him out of his own house, which they were then busy plundering. As I stood commiserating his misfortunes, and ashamed of the rapacity and cruelty exercised by my countrymen, two of the 88th Connaught Rangers made their appearance, who coming forward, audaciously demanded from the Spaniard his money. The poor man solemnly protested he had none; that they might perceive he had no means of secreting anything about his person; that his all was gone; his house had been robbed and plundered; his property carried away and destroyed; himself stripped and turned out of the house, which called him master, and into which he durst not enter, as it was still occupied by the deprecators.'

Brown's disgust at the actions of the British soldiers was made even more so when he entered a house where he was relieved to see that the occupants, an old woman and a child were unharmed as the British soldiers, merrily pillaging and getting intoxicated surrounding them paid them no attention. However when he rounded into the next room he was appalled to see that a score of British soldiers were in jubilation around the body of a young woman, clearly the child's mother.

'One fellow held up in triumph a pair of red morocco boots he had torn from her feet; while another wretch displayed a rich necklace he had stripped from her bosom. But I turned from the revolting scene in disgust, and rushed out of this most unfortunate and ruined house.'

It took Wellington three days to restore order to his disorganized forces, at the cost of many floggings and hangings to set an example to those who may have larceny or worse in their hearts. Cuidad Rodrigo had cost Wellington 105 men killed and 390 wounded, a comparatively low figure for such an operation of this nature. Badajoz however had a more costly figure. Of the 26,950 men in Wellingtons forces used to besiege the city, 3,500 had been killed or wounded, many burned and disfigured in the intense heat and closeness of the battle. Amongst his wounded, Badajoz also cost Wellington five of his best generals, including Sir Thomas Picton, who was invalided out leaving his beloved Division in the hands of Sir Thomas Pakenham.

The cost was so terrible that on the morning of 7 April Wellington wept as he stood on the breach of the Trinidad and looked out onto the remains of his shattered columns.

In his dispatches to Lord Liverpool he also commented that;

'The capture of Badajoz affords as strong an instance of gallantry of our troops as has ever been displayed. But I realty [sic] hope that I shall never again be the instrument of putting them to such a test…'

The shambles that had been the entire preparation and carrying out of the assault on the fortress walls finally demonstrated to the Army chiefs in Whitehall that if he were to conduct a successful siege, Wellington desperately required a proper siege train in the Peninsula and so the new Corps of Engineers and Sappers was formed and dispatched in mid 1813 to efficiently carry out the surveying and digging of siege work.

Though the new Corps and siege train found themselves employed once again at San Sebastian and Burgos in 1813, these sieges were very quick and bloodless in comparison to the nightmare that was Cuidad Rodrigo and Badajoz. Wellington's request came true and he would never again have to throw men at the walls in such a manner. Due to the proper resources sent to him to conduct sieges, this also no longer caused the infantry to enter a fortress full of vengeance and desire. In short, Cuidad Rodrigo and Badajoz were costly lesson to learn, but lessons that would never be forgotten to future generations.

The Offensive Continues

— Salamanca — Vittoria — San Sebastian — Pyrennean Campaign — Nive — Nivelle - Toulouse

Following the fall of the two great fortresses, Wellington rested his army and brought up the provisions to his new major stores from which he could now launch his offensive into Spain. In order to keep an eye on enemy action he sent Rowland Hill's division to attack and seize a pontoon bridge at Almaraz that was protected by a French garrison in the aptly named Fort Napoleon. During a desperate fight on 19 May 19, Hill's men succeeded in capturing the fort and thus gained control of an integral river crossing point, managing to sever the communications between Marmont and Soult across the Tagus.

Wellington's biggest obstacle facing him in central Spain was that of Marshal Marmont's 52,000 strong force. Though Wellington had 60,000 men at his disposal, he had no other hand to play whilst Marmont could call reinforcements from King Joseph. Napoleon's army was still at a further disadvantage as he had removed most of the forces occupying Spain, including his beloved Guards, to attack Russia. Seizing the opportunity to attack whilst the French were incapable of strong resistance, Wellington marched on Marmont's force at Salamanca on 13 June with 48,000 men and 54 guns, knowing he could not hope to make a strong defence. Marmont withdrew from the area leaving Wellington to march in victoriously on 17 June. Both armies were now encamped either side of the River Guardania and by 21 June both armies had crossed the River Tormes and were encamped so close to each other that the men could shout to each other and fraternizations became common place. On 22 July the armies faced each other over a plain broken only by two hills, the Greater Arapile, occupied by Marmont and the Lesser Arapile, occupied by Wellington.

Very little happened on the morning as both armies were still trying to out manoeuvre each other, but around midday Wellington noticed that Thomieres 7th Division had managed to outstrip his own forces and was threatening to flank his leading column. To prevent them from coming round he ordered the 3rd Division under Pakenham to attack, with the 45th at the head of the attacking force commanded by Lt. Col. Ridewood. Thomieres division was largely strung out on the road to Cuidad Rodrigo when the 3rd Division attacked. The 6,000 strong British and Portuguese division caused mass panic in Thomieres division as they fired well-practiced volley after volley into the loose ranks causing over 3,000 French casualties including Thomieres himself, until finally the French ranks broke and fled in panic. As the French were breaking a French officer found himself with a clear shot at Pakenham, by some form of grace the pistol misfired, but not giving the Frenchman a chance to reload a corporal of the 45th sprang forward bayonet fixed and shot the officer, an act that saw the unfortunate redcoat killed himself. Had this man's act not succeeded, Pakenham could well have been another casualty listed on the field that day. The French cavalry counter attacked this move and began to swarm around the 45th's ranks. General Pakenham happened to be riding passed just as the 45$_{th}$'s Grenadier Company unleashed a staggering volley into the attacking cavalry causing the General to cry out *'Well done 45th!'* The cavalry were soon sent packing.

Elsewhere the French had almost succeeded in shifting the 12,000 British defenders from the Lesser Arapile, but fortunately the stubbornness, determination and seasoned firepower of the defenders sent their attackers reeling back down the slopes in disarray.

The sight of Thomieres retreating men caused other regiments to panic and flee the field, some before they had even come to battle, others that had become engaged found they could not break the British position and were being meted out the same punishment. The French attack and overall position finally broke when a cavalry charge by British dragoons finally broke the French ranks and also their spirit for the fight. Salamanca had cost Wellington 5,214 casualties; the French rate was much higher being 14,000 with 20 guns captured. The 45th had lost five killed, with Major Greenwell, Lt. Col. Forbes, Capt. Lightfoot, Lt. Coghlan, Ensign Rey, one sergeant and forty-four rank and file wounded. Greenwell, who was shot three times yet maintained the command of his troops was to receive the CB for his conduct on the field. Greenwell's CB was not the only honour to be bestowed on the 45th that day, for now Wellington had a clear path to Madrid and when he marched into the Spanish capital on 12 August, it was the band of the 45th, proudly playing the *British Grena*diers marching at the head of the conquering column.

Following their glorious and exuberant entrance into the Spanish capital, Wellington now turned his attentions to another fortified town of Burgos, which controlled the road from the Ebro Valley to the Duoro. Leaving his most seasoned divisions, including 'The Fighting Third' at Madrid to guard the line of the Tagus, Wellington marched on Burgos with some 23,000 men, which included Pack's Portuguese and the 1st, 5th and 7th Divisions on 18 September to shift the 2,200 strong garrison. With only the 18 pounders to hand and again lacking any adequate resources in sappers or miners, Wellington's assault of the fortress ultimately failed and under the cover of darkness on 21 October 1812, Wellington pulled his forces back at the cost of 2,000 men.

With Wellington now in full retreat, Soult's cavalry continually harassed the retreating British forces as they disconsolately wound their way southwest. The 52,000 Anglo/Portuguese army accompanied by 18,000 Spanish were by this time exhausted from the last few months of campaigning and found that there was little food or rations to be had, owing to the fact that the French had plundered the earth or it had been razed to the ground by the Allies to prevent it from falling into enemy hands. French cavalry swarmed everywhere, picking off stragglers or seizing prisoners. Over 1,600 prisoners were taken including Sir Edward Paget, who was captured by three dragoons and was rendered unable to fight them off after losing his arm at Oporto. In conditions mirroring that of the retreat to Corruna, the British forces were dishevelled, weary, half starved, and ill-equipped, this cost them some 3,000 men during the retreat into Portugal. By 28 November the British forces were scattered all over the Iberia with communications made difficult due to the terrain and routes.

The winter of late 1812, early 1813 enabled Wellington's forces to recover after the manic year of 1812. Re-clothed, well fed and with fresh determination, 1813 looked to be the year that Wellington would push further into Spain. The 2/59th returned to the Iberian Peninsula in August 1812 and were ordered to lift the French siege at Cadiz. They arrived too late to assist in the siege and spent the next six months on garrison duty there. In spring 1813 they sailed out to Lisbon to join Wellington's forces massing there in a fresh attempt to break out into Spain.

Wellington spent no time brooding the failures towards the end of 1812 and instead reorganized his staff to bring in fresh ideas and a new determination in invading Spain. News that the French morale had sunk further still due to Napoleon's failure in Russia and he was pulling troops out of Spain at an alarming rate to boost defence across Europe, reached Wellington in January, and by May 1813 he had almost 70,000 men at his disposal, an extra 12,000 Spanish and 106 guns compared to the estimated 80,000–100,000 French occupying the Portuguese border. To confuse the French Wellington sent 30,000 men under Sir Rowland Hill to central Spain where the French expected the main advance to come from. However, in a move the French were oblivious to, Wellington had 60,000 men, including the 2/59th, under the command of Sir Thomas Graham cross the Duoro further south in preparation for the allied break out, which lured Joseph Bonaparte north of Burgos with a force of 60,000. This came on 22 May when Wellington advanced into Spain with all of his 80,000 men now across the Duoro. Legend has it that crossing the border Wellington turned his horse, raised his hat and called out, *'Farewell, Portugal, for I shall never see you again'*. If there was ever such a premonition, this was it.

The French, panicking at the allied sudden appearance from right under their noses, were forced to abandon Burgos but not before blowing the fortress walls up to prevent them from being used by the allies. Wellington ordered supply ships to be brought up to supply his troops, as they rushed to beat the French march on him. Wellington ordered that all troops only carry with them what they could and keep wagons to a minimum, at one point during the march the 59th received a tongue lashing from the General when he discovered the regiment dragging a cart loaded with private baggage.

Wellington finally caught up with the French at Vittoria, which lay some six miles wide and ten miles long along the valley floor of the Zadorra with heights running all along it's edge. In an elaborate show of might, Wellington split his forces into four columns with Hill on the right and the 3rd Division forming one of the central columns (with the 45th on their extreme right), which Wellington assumed personal command of, were to advance through the valley of Bayas northwest of the battlefield.

Around 8:30am Hill's troops attacked the French forcing them to abandon their position on the heights, two hours later Graham's force swept down the mountains to cut off their escape route on the valley floor. The 3rd Division were ordered to assault the bridge over the Mendoza and led by the 45th, successfully crossed only to find themselves facing two French divisions and heavy artillery opposition. The guns were promptly silenced by Kempt's rifle brigade and forced to retire. At 3pm the 3rd, 7th and Light Divisions became engaged with the French holding the village of Margarita which represented a crucial position to the right of the French line. Despite facing heavy French opposition the 3rd Division held on so stolidly that the French defenders were eventually routed. The 45th also helped to attack the village of Ariniz and engaged the French in bitter hand to hand fighting in a combat that closely echoed the narrow street fighting of Buenos Aires and Fuentes d'Onoro. With stiff determination, the 45th eventually managed to dislodge their opposition and sent them streaming out of the village.

The 59th, comprising of Robinson's Brigade along with the 4th and 47th was tasked with taking Gamorra-Mayor, a small village that overlooked the British crossing point with an integral bridge crossing to the French side of the river. The three regiments attacked the village in three columns under the fire of the French guns that forced their march into a run. Coming upon the village they halted, fired a devastating volley into the French troops holding the village then launched a bayonet charge headlong, jumping the defences and sweeping away all resistance. Their victory was short lived however and the French brought forward a dozen guns to fire onto the village. The French infantry stormed back over the bridge forcing Robinson's brigade further back into the village. Though the bridge was back in French hands now, the village remained under British control forcing a stalemate where neither side could press home the attack.

With the French right now swept clean away, a fresh British attack by Cole's 4th Division at 5pm eventually snapped the French centre and forced a wedge between the two central French divisions resulting in mass panic as the French column began to crumble and flee with the French troops throwing away all equipment and baggage in a bid to make their escape faster. An hour later those French that had not fled attempted to make a brave stand in front of Vittoria, but again the 3rd Division were close at hand and routed this last attempt to hold the ground.

In the crush and mêlée to flee the battlefield much of the French baggage was left behind. Amidst the tents, provisions and stores was also the French wagon train consisting of 100 wagons, 151 guns and 415 ammunition caissons. Most infamously amid these wagons was the royal treasure of Joseph Bonaparte, King of Spain and Napoleon's eldest brother. Not quite content with seeing the French off the battlefield, the British pursued their prey in frenzy, mercilessly cutting down French stragglers and fugitives. The only saving grace for the French was that the British only stopped in their complete rampage to plunder the wagon park.

The 45th took light casualties at Vittoria with only four rank and file killed. A further 61 other ranks were wounded along with four officers and five sergeants. Most unfortunately, one of these officers mentioned was Lt. Col. Ridewood who died of wounds received, the following day.

Maj. Gen. Brisbane, who commanded the 1st brigade of the 3rd Division to which the 45th belonged later commented that;

'The Major-General cannot help lamenting that the 45th and the service should have been deprived of the able assistance of so valuable an officer as Lieut. Col. Ridewood, in consequence of his wounds, received at the termination of so glorious an action.'

The attack and action around Gamarro-Mayor had cost Robinson's Brigade 500 dead and wounded of which 160 were from the 59th. Amongst the 59th casualty list was Lt. Col. Fane who had been wounded in the thigh by a cannon ball and subsequently died of his wounds a few days later.

The overall casualty list for Vittoria stood at 5,100 Allied, a third of this number attributes to the 3rd Division whose persistence and relentlessness brought them heavily into combat with the enemy, to 8,000 French losses.

The British victory at Vittoria marked the beginning of the end for the French occupation of Spain. Until now, the French had thought themselves invincible on the battlefield, even with incurring major defeats such as Salamanca and Talavera, they had always believed that they would be able to drive the British from the Iberian Peninsula if they held out long enough. Vittoria, however, now demonstrated that the British forces were strengthening and the cataclysmic loss of Joseph Bonaparte's royal treasure combined with the broken army returning from Russia now demonstrated to Napoleon that his army was not as invincible as he had led himself to believe.

Wellington, now seen as a thorn in Bonaparte's side, was reluctant to pursue the French any further into Spain until he was sure of the general situation of French defeat elsewhere in Europe. Once he was ready to advance he had the dilemma of overstretching his supply line straight from Lisbon. This meant that he now needed to find another strong costal port further into Spain if he was going to make a 'big push' into France. His main options were to his north the fortress of San Sebastian, to his south the strongly held fortified town of Pampelona. Taking the more obvious route Wellington opted to take San Sebastian.

San Sebastian was in prime position to cover the Bay of Biscay and controlled the major river ports. In order to push home his advance Wellington would be able to use San Sebastian as a depot for his advance parties and also receive provisions and equipment from home.

By mid July the siege work was well underway and San Sebastian was cut off from receiving any reinforcements. The British troops at San Sebastian first of all captured the monastery at San Bartolomeo. The monastery occupied high ground and from here the first batteries were laid to bombard the gigantic curtain wall in the east surrounding the medieval city. San Sebastian was the first siege to be laid after Badajoz and Cuidad Rodrigo in early 1812. Learning from the high casualties and bloodshed San Sebastian was besieged in the proper manner where the newly established Corps of Sappers and Miners, a special branch of the Royal Engineers, were brought in to properly oversee the besieging works. Wellington now also had the luxury of a proper siege train and adequate ammunition that was brought up by boat close to the besieging camp. The French occasionally would fire back onto the ever-encroaching trenches and even launch attacks to drive back the besiegers. One such incident occurred during the night of 25 July when the 59th, holding the

British trenches found themselves under heavy fire from French artillery in the city and sustained 30 casualties. Fearing another long, drawn out siege like Badajoz, Wellington ordered up more guns, supplies and ammunition and re-commenced a heavy barrage on the city walls.

On the night of 26 August the 59th and 200 men of the 9th regiment launched an attack and captured the island of Santa Clara from which more batteries and trenches could be dug to bombard the Western side of San Sebastian. The next day Major General Leith took command of the 5th Division from Oswald and was given the task of finding 750 volunteers from 1st, 4th and Light Division to assault the main breach alongside the 5th Division who were to be led by the Light Companies of Robinson's Brigade.

The attack was planned for 11am on 31 August. Whilst Wellington would have liked a night assault he could only guarantee that the tide would be out in the daytime allowing troops to circle the walls into the shallow rock pools. The assault began with an attack by Lieutenant Francis Maguire of the 4th leading the Forlorn Hope and a party of 12 men of the mining party who hoped to blow the mines hidden in the breach. Half of the Forlorn Hope including Maguire were decimated when the defenders blew the mines in the breach but their sacrifice meant that the attacking columns no longer had to fear hidden mines in the rubble.

Robinson's Brigade attacked in two columns, one to assault he main breach directly and the other to tackle the curtain wall to its right. Reaching the top of the wall the men found themselves faced with a thin piece of wall to gain a foothold and facing them a well defended inner wall, heavily manned and pouring musket fire onto the outer wall, between them was a 30 foot drop lined with the murderous chevrex-des-frise, blocks of wood with sword blades sticking out designed to rip and snag unaware attackers.

Once over the walls and through the breach the attackers had little option but to navigate their way over the walls and across the ramparts, all the while having masonry falling on them from exploding mines and in a hail of bullets form the defenders. The Light Companies took the brunt of the attack and the 59th especially lost most of its Light Company officers in the first wave. As the remnants of the first wave began to climb the walls and hold back the enemy the rest of the battalions followed to support them. Not all mines had been blown and Captain Scott, leading the 59th and a number of officers and men were killed when a mine was exploded in front of them that the first wave had managed to avoid.

To alleviate the pressure on the troops in the breaches, Wellington ordered that the siege guns fire over the heads of the attackers onto the bastions pouring fire into the breaches. Using this 'creeping barrage' type tactic, Wellington was able to silence the guns housed in the bastions and allow more troops to be brought up under the cover of fire. One lucky shell rolled down a chimney straight into a powder magazine. The explosion rocked the defenders and killed hundreds of them outright. The fire on the breaches had also eased off and men were now able to make it over the obstacles and into the city, where what started as a trickle of a lucky few soon became a swarm of British troops overrunning the French positions and fighting hand to hand to secure every alley and street.

Many troops became separated from their own regiments and companies in the assault on the breaches. The 59th managed to join up with a mixture of British and Portuguese troops who had entered through another breach in the walls and began to flush out the pockets of resistance.

In an aftermath similar to that of Badajoz and Cuidad Rodrigo, the British army went on a rampage of looting and drinking. Private John Russell of the 59th witnessed a soldier attempt to take a pocket watch from a dead officer of the 59th. Levelling his musket at the man's chest he warned him away and saved the watch. The carnage was only brought to a halt and order regained when a giant storm broke out a few hours after the fall of the town and dampened the men's spirits. Not all of San Sebastian had fallen and the Castle still remained in French hands. Wellington ordered that the Castle be bombarded from the first to third of September and lifted the barrage on the fourth so negotiations could be carried out. However the French effort to postpone the surrender only saw Wellington order up more batteries and continue the bombardment until the Castle officially surrendered on 8 September.

Though the casualty list was not as devastating as the sieges in early 1812, San Sebastian had nonetheless sustained a long list of killed and wounded. Overall 856 were killed and 1,520 wounded. Amongst the dead was Colonel Fletcher, who had orchestrated the sieges of Badajoz and Cuidad Rodrigo, General Oswald and General Leith the commanders of the 5th Division had both been hit and so had General Robinson whose Brigade had led the assault and now only stood at 43% in strength. The 59th had suffered 350 casualties and seen its Light Company practically destroyed in the assault.

Despite Wellington's reservations about the effectiveness of the 5th Division in the beginning, General Robinson highly praised the 59th in a report to General Ross, the 59th's Colonel in England. Robinson said of the 59th;

'Nothing could exceed the intrepidity of the Regiment. It rushed forward cheering and gained the top of the breach under a fire that threatened the destruction of the whole party.'

He would also go on to call the 59th an 'ornament to the British Army.'

The siege of San Sebastian was one of the last great sieges of the Peninsular War. In taking the town and castle Wellington had now secured a port close to the French border in which he could start massing supplies ready for his big offensive later that year.

Elsewhere during the besieging of San Sebastian, Wellington also had to keep harrying the French to prevent their forces from meeting up and turning on him. Pursuing as cautiously as he could, Wellington had swept the French out of the vast plains of Spain but was now tasked with chasing them through the mountains. The summer months of 1813 now became a string of minor engagements that became known as the Battle of the Pyrenees. Emulating the actions in the rough Portuguese terrain of 1809, Wellington only had the option of choosing the major routes that ran past Ronscavelles and Maya that could accommodate his supply wagons and artillery train. Soult, now in charge of 114,000 French troops decided to make a stand in these mountains, and seeing that the Allied army, consisting of just little over 82,000 in total, were broken up over the mountains to cover all routes, decided to destroy them piecemeal. The British, numbering some 20,000 found themselves attacked by six French divisions, numbering a vast 35,000 at Ronscavelles. The British, drawn up on their ridge, managed to hold their ground and drive off the densely packed columns as they struggled to navigate over the rocky terrain. A thick fog descended over the battlefield bringing it to an inconclusive end with the French falling back to stronger positions, and Cole's 10,000 strong force falling back to the Pamplona Road towards Sorauen and just behind the ridge, Picton's 3rd Division was ready to defend the Ronscavelles – Pamplona Road.

On the morning of 28 July, Wellington was awaiting Pack's force to arrive along the Pamplona road at Sorauen, when a French force arrived to threaten Wellington's position. In timely arrival Pack's force were immediately engaged and managed to close in on the French force and drive them back. Wellington, a tactical mastermind as ever, came to rely heavily on the steep slopes and broken ground of the terrain to break up the advancing columns and make the packed ranks easy targets for his established superior firepower. Despite holding their ground, the thin British skirmish line holding the ridge was soon overwhelmed by the persistent French force and began to waiver. With the crest now wide open the French pressed home their advance seeing a clear gap. However, as they reached the crest two British battalions sprang forward from the ground and poured devastating volley fire into the French ranks followed home with a mass bayonet charge. Already thrown into confusion and panic, the French turned and fled back down the slopes. In the dense paths and packed terrain, the casualties were quite high for a minor engagement that lasted only half a day. The French had suffered over 4,000 casualties whilst the Allied list stood at 2,658. On 30

July Soult's men streamed northwards from their higher positions leaving a force to hold Sorauen. Wellington's artillery opened fire on the retreating forces and in a combined assault British swept down onto the French left flank to engage the remaining French manning the barricades. The result was a mass rout in which those French who stayed at their posts were butchered to the last man.

Whilst Soult's forces were engaged in the Pyrenees, Graham's forces were still laying siege to the costal fortification of San Sebastian. At noon on 31 August the Allied troops were ordered to storm the breaches made by their artillery since siege operations began on 28 June the same year. In events similar to that of Badajoz and Cuidad Rodrigo, the British were repulsed in several places but their persistence finally allowed them to break through and defeat the defenders. Also in shameless fashion, the besiegers went on a rampage of looting and drunkenness this time only curbed by a massive fire that engulfed the town. Allied losses however were a lot fewer than had been incurred at the two great sieges at the start of 1812. Both Cuidad Rodrigo and Badajoz had shown Wellington that he needed proper siege equipment and engineering experts to avoid such losses and tragedy. San Sebastian, due to its location along the coast rather than inland, and Wellington's persistent letters to Horse Guards and Whitehall, afforded him proper siege guns sent from England by boat to Passages for San Sebastian and also a proper engineering arm sent out to him to conduct the siege properly.

Following the fall of San Sebastian and sensing impending failure in Spain, Soult's army was desperate to pull back into France to reorganize themselves and replenish their losses. They were still fighting a bitter rear-guard action against the pursuing British forces that were gradually pushing through the Pyrenees towards the River Bidossa, the border between Spain and France. The 45th found themselves encamped between the mountain passes of Echalar and Maya, where in the high terrain they were exposed to heavy rains and torrential snowstorms. The long months of toiling and the fractured communication lines and poor mountain roads also meant that provisions were few, if any arrived at all, and they were also continually harassed by French scouting and cavalry parties.

At a place called Vera, the French were checked in their retreat by a Captain Cadaoux of the 95th Rifles who held the bridge with just one company of riflemen for over two hours causing 231 enemy casualties that included the French General Vandermassen. Following Cadaoux's retreat the French crossed the Bidossa to the safety of the other side and back on French soil. On 7 October Wellington finally crossed the bridge into France, in the face of heavy opposition taking 1,200 casualties. Now in the land of his enemy, Wellington turned his attentions to dealing with the French who had entrenched themselves in fortified positions along the River Nivelle. Facing him was an army that stretched from the Atlantic shore to Ronscavelles high up in the Pyrenean passes. Reflecting the formidable Lines of Torres Vedras from 1810–11 the hills and natural landscape created natural obstacles and difficulties for the attacking forces, which the defenders had strengthened with artillery placements and blockhouses. Though this line of defence was manned by over 63,000 troops, they were incredibly stretched over 20 miles in the face of Wellington's 80,000 strong force who could be concentrated in just one area along this stretch. Wellington's plan was to assault the whole line probing for weaknesses, but placed a special emphasis on attacking the centre in a bid to split the defences into two halves and then flank them from the north where they were weakest. Wellington left his central forces under the command of Sir William Carr Beresford, amongst them were 'The Fighting Third' to make plans to assault the centre head on.

The Light Division were selected to attack the steep slopes of La Rhune, a rocky slope some 2,800 feet high, and clear the area to open the French flank up to an attack. The French were caught completely unaware of any attack and fearing a larger British force were completely routed and fled in panic.

With the flank now exposed the 3rd Division now attacked the centre, securing the bridge at Amotz and taking the heights to the left, thus succeeding in splitting Soult's communication lines and causing his position to collapse. With no idea of what was happening, Soult's forces panicked and began to dwindle away to re-connect with each other. By 2pm on 30 November they were in a complete shambles having lost all contact with the Staff.

The splitting of Soult's communications had come at a great cost though, British casualties stood at 2,450, of which the 45th made up one tenth of this number and the French had lost 4,351.

Wellington's victory at the Nivelle was short lived as Soult pulled his troops back to Bayonne. For the majority of the war Bayonne had been acting as the integral French depot for all forces in Spain, the stores had been painstakingly built up over the years, the garrison was strong, and the city defences were impenetrable. More important was that the population was loyal to Napoleon, Wellington's army if they were not careful, were liable to be open to the same civilian hostilities faced by the French in Spain. Fearing that the Spanish troops would extract some form of revenge in France, Wellington took the painful decision to send them back to defend the Spanish border, as some Spanish atrocities to the French peasantry had already occurred.

Faced with another obstacle, Wellington now had to cross his troops over the River Nive in order to assault Bayonne. On 9 December the 3rd Division, under Beresford, were instructed to cross the Nive on the right by a pontoon bridge at Ustaritz. However, heavy French resistance on Wellington's left, that consisted of small actions between 10 and 13 December forced the British from their positions. As this delayed the British advance into Bayonne, the 3rd and 4th Division were ordered to cross the Nive to alleviate pressure on Hill. Unfortunately the heavy rains had swept away the intended pontoon bridge on 12 December and Beresford was unable to bring his support up. The Count d'Erlon committed 50,000 troops to the village of Anglet to sweep away the 30,000 of the 1st and 5th Divisions. The 2/59th, leading Oswald's 5th Division, held Soult' forces off long enough for Wellington to bring up reinforcements at Anglet. Their stubborn defence cost them 159 casualties but had prevented the French forces from breaking through and splitting the British force in half. Hill became embroiled in a savage assault by 35,000 French at St. Pierre, which almost cost him dearly. However, he put up a strong defence until the 4th and 3rd Division, by using the pontoon bridge at Villafranca, managed to come to his aid. Hostilities ceased on 13 December, with Soult pulling back his forces closer to Bayonne. Though neither side had gained an advantage, Wellington was now securely on French soil. With 1,500 Allied casualties to the 3,500 French, the campaign of 1813 came to an end as both armies encamped for the winter, the 45th being stationed around Campo. The Battle of the Nive was to be the 2/59th's last engagement of the war.

Having sat out the winter in relative comfort, Bayonne still was growing stronger and was still providing to the armed forces. Wellington began to plan his next move and between 23 and 26 February 1814, he set about blockading Bayonne by launching a crossing across the Ardour, sending the 3rd Division to occupy the river at Berenx to defend against any relief, and surrounding the north of the city – preventing any provisions and supplies from getting out or in.

On 27 February, when Wellington caught up with Soult, he had 38,000 infantry, 3,300 cavalry and 54 guns to Soult's slightly outnumbered force who made up for their losses by drawing up onto a strong position on a ridge.

The 4th Division launched the opening of the attack by assaulting the French at the village of St Boes. Whilst this left the French distracted, the 3rd Division attacked Soult's centre taking heavy losses from the French artillery, sweeping the fractured and broken ground that forced the men to advance slowly and cautiously up. The 45th were positioned to the rear of the division and at one point Wellington, who was reconnoitring the ground, saw a gap in the line which could lead the French to launch an attack if they thought the ground was unopposed, rode up to Lt. Munro of the 45th and ordered: *'Get the other side of the hill, or the enemy will see that that there are no more troops across, and will be down on us!'*

At 11:30am Wellington ordered a general advance along the whole front with the 3rd Division pushing its way up the eastern spur supported closely by the 6th Division. From their strong position the French were able to hold off the attacks causing heavy losses to the allies, in an ironic twist of fate the forces had seemed to switch their preferred tactic. French cavalry charges also caused devastating losses amongst the 88th who were only saved by the rest of the 3rd Division.

Seeking another way onto the French positions the British began to construct a pontoon bridge across the Gave de Pau at Bereux for which the 3rd Division were to cross. The 45th, at the head of the division, were the first across and advanced in line up a more practicable slope coming face to face with the French defenders on their ridge. Here they engaged with the French slugging it out exchanging volley's, but neither side willing to budge. It was only when the 45th's and other Light Company's from the division, with elements of the 60th Rifles began to cause damage that the line began to weaken.

It was only by chance that the 52nd managed to take the French force in the flank and caused the position to fall. Seeing their comrades retreat, other parts of the line began to panic and fall back, soon the whole of Soult's line was in full retreat towards Toulouse.

This action had cost the 3rd Division some 70 officers and 800 men lost. The 45th had lost Lt. Col. Forbes and Lt. Col. Greenwell badly wounded whilst leading the Light Infantry into their attack, two Lieutenants were killed and one captain and three lieutenants wounded. The most tragic casualty that day was Lt. MacPherson, the hero of Badajoz, who, attempting to rally his men, got in the way of a French volley where he was so badly wounded that he had to be invalided out of the army. By no doubt the 3rd Division had suffered the highest casualty rate in the British army at Orthez. The total casualty rate cost Wellington, who was slightly wounded himself at the battle, 2,164 men, Soult suffering 4,000 with 1,350 men taken prisoner.

The Battle of Orthez brought the British forces one step closer to finally conquering their French nemesis of six years, they were now in their enemy's country but there were still a few obstacles to overcome. Following Orthez, Wellington and Soult clashed frequently in skirmishes and small actions as the British vanguard came close to the French rear-guard. The 45th were engaged in one such event at Vic Bigore when the 3rd Division managed to drive two divisions from their positions on 17 March.

Bordeaux, the major French port in the south, fell to Allies on 12 March, enabling Wellington to now re-direct his supplies and provisions straight into France rather than over the mountains. Wellington now turned his attentions to the 'walled city' of Toulouse, the last major city before Paris. In besieging the city the allies placed their siege artillery on the Calvinet Ridge, a series of heights some 600 feet high from which they could bombard the city. A series of attempts to take the city ensued, on 4 April, Beresford with 19,000 men including the 3rd Division, half of Wellington's force, crossed the River Garonne on newly constructed pontoon bridges. Unfortunately, in events echoing Orthez the heavy rains swept the pontoons away mid crossing leaving Beresford stranded on the enemy side. Had Soult wanted to attack he would have succeeded in butchering all caught between the riverbank and the city walls. Soult however, was cautious and made no move to pick off the enemy in their fragile state, giving Wellington time to reconstruct the pontoons, and four days later on 8 April all of the British force had crossed bar Hill's Corps who remained on the left bank of the Garonne to cover a retreat if necessary. On 10 April the 3rd and Light Divisions were instructed to attack along the line of the Languedoc Canal to the north of the city. This done, Picton got over-zealous and ordered Brisbane's brigade, to which the 45th belonged, to march on the bridge over the canal to take some farm buildings and orchards. This order was not thoroughly considered as the brigade took heavy losses due to stronger resistance than anticipated.

Elsewhere in the fight for the city, Freire's Spanish brigade came under heavy artillery fire positioned on the Calvinet Ridge. The brigade, seeking shelter from the rain of shot and shell, took cover in a sunken lane but found themselves caught between French infantry to their front and flanking artillery. Trapped between volley fire and close range canister, the brigade took heavy casualties and were only saved by a British attack on Mont Rave to distract the French artillery so the Spaniards stood a chance of fighting their way out.

The 4th and 6th Divisions were also having luck as they managed to take part of the Calvinet Ridge from the enemy and hold if from any counter-attacks. During this engagement, Picton launched another attack on the north of the city but again was beaten back suffering 354 casualties, amongst that number were the 1st Brigade's commander, Sir Thomas Brisbane, and the 45th's very own Col. Forbes. Just a little before nightfall the 6th Division managed to prise Soult off the Calvinet Ridge, but not before incurring heavy losses.

The next day the French abandoned Toulouse to its fate and headed for Carassone. On 14 April General Thouvenot, commander of Bayonne launched a desperate attack on his British besiegers, costing him 905 men. Again the British command structure took two casualties in the form of Sir John Hope, wounded and captured, and General Hay, along with 838 men. Three days later on 17 April, with Napoleon nowhere to be seen, Marshal Soult, Duke of Dalmatia, was tasked with negotiating the armistice, bringing the conflict that had raged over three countries in six years to a close. Sadder still was that the Battle of Toulouse had been needlessly fought. Napoleon had abdicated at 2pm on 31 March and Paris had surrendered to the Prussians, Austrians and Russians. News of this only reached Wellington a few days after Toulouse fell. Wellington, in a style not normally associated with such an austere and cold character, reportedly snapped his fingers and performed a little jig on the spot crying, *'You don't say so! 'Pon my honour! Hurrah!'*

The Battle of Toulouse had needlessly cost Wellington 4,568 troops, the French, 3,236. Within this number the 3rd Division had taken yet another high casualty toll with Col Forbes and seven rank and file killed, one major, one captain, five lieutenants, one ensign and 69 rank and file wounded.

So to came the end of French occupation in the Peninsula, and with it the end of a long and drawn out war that had spread over five continents. Estimates and calculations show that Wellington's veteran battalions like the 45th who had been with him since the army first landed at Mondego Bay in 1808 had marched 6,000 miles in advances and retreats all over the Iberian Peninsula.

Now most of these regiments were to be split from their divisions and sent to different areas of the world. Only a few chosen regiments would be allowed to stay in France for when the British entered Paris. Others were to be posted back home to England, some to the

West Indies; others were going straight from one conflict zone to another to assist in quelling the rebellious Americans across the Atlantic who had been waging a fresh war with Great Britain since 1812. Estimates say that 40,000 British alone lost their lives in the Peninsula – only one quarter of this was due to enemy action, the rest was through fever, disease, hunger and cold.

The 45th, who had stayed with Wellington every step of the Peninsula Campaign were mustered at Grenade 16 miles from Toulouse under acting Lt. Col. Greenwell, who had been a mere junior Captain on landing at Mondego Bay in 1808. They were then issued orders to march to Bordeaux where on 15 June they were reviewed by Wellington one last time. Sir Thomas Picton, who had commanded 'The Fighting Third' through some of its toughest engagements also bid farewell to his beloved Division at Bordeaux.

The 45th were to board transports to Ireland where they landed at Monkstown on 23 and 24 July 1814. From here they marched to their barracks at Enniskillin with a strength of 44 sergeants, 22 drummers and 694 rank and file. Soon after, the battalions found themselves being broken up and men either discharged or sent to fight in other regiments. With the ranks broken up the regiment had remarkably managed to hold onto both their colours that had flown over the ranks in every engagement. By the end of the Peninsula Campaign the flags were tattered and torn to shreds by shot, sabre, and shell. They had long since lost their original poles and were instead tied to poles fashioned from the branches of Spanish hedgerows. Following the disbandment of the 2nd Battalion the 1st Battalion were given their colours and legend has it that the colours they had so proudly carried through Portugal, Spain and France were burned unceremoniously in a Belfast barrack square.

The 2/59th were also sent to Ireland where in a similar state to the 45th, they were to undertake garrison and civil duties.

For both regiments, their rest in Ireland was to be short lived however as in late February 1815 the battalion received news that Napoleon Bonaparte, once the scourge of all Europe had escaped his exile on the tiny Mediterranean island of Elba and was sweeping through France, building an army. Wellington, now a celebrated figure across Europe and a commander of just a few guards regiments in Brussels, was tasked once again with commanding a medley army of British, Germans, Dutch, allied with the Prussians, that were to stop Napoleon.

News on this fresh outbreak of war reached the 45th and 59th who were instructed to sail for the Low Countries as reinforcements. The 2/59th sailed to Kent and from there to Ostend where they came ashore on 3 May 1815.

WATERLOO CAMPAIGN

Waterloo was Napoleon's last throw of the dice in his gamble for European dominance, as the armies of the major European powers crammed into the Belgian countryside to do battle one last time.

The allies held the Brussels Road with the main force lining the ridge of Mont St Jean. The ridge sloped down into a valley, which was fronted by three farmsteads, on the right, the Chateau of Hougoumont, in the centre La Haye Saint and to the left, Pappellotte. Wellington's strategy was to funnel the French army onto the ridge between the farmsteads but using these to pour flanking fire into the French columns, the main allied force on the ridge would then finish off the French advance once their shattered remnants had reached their positions.

The 2/59th were quartered at Oudenared and comprised part of Colville's 4th Division in Johnstone's Brigade alongside the 2/35th, 1/54th and 1/91st.

The French attack was delayed until mid morning owing to heavy rainfall on the evening of 17 June, Napoleon's artillery commanders were hesitant to move their guns into position whilst the ground was soaked. The ground had dried out by 11am and the French attack began. The French attack concentrated on Hougoumont on the right, Napoleon's plan was to bombard the Chateau, take it and use it as a launch pad to flank the allied line.

Fighting in the claustrophobic conditions of the Chateau was Private Matthew Clay of the 3rd Foot Guards. Hailing from Blidworth near Mansfield. Clay's regiment had encountered the French at Quatre Bras two days before, where they had beaten back the French offensive but had then been forced to retreat. Whist his regiment was positioned to the right of Wellington's flank, Clay's company was placed into the Chateau of Hougoumont to add strength to the Guards units already there. The main French attack, rather than just march past the Chateau, turned and attacked directly. For twelve hours Clay was confined within the chateau walls as the garrison fought desperately to prevent the French from entering. The chateau almost fell in the first attack when a giant French sapper identified as *Sous-lieutenant* (Junior lieutenant) Legros, smashed open the gates with his axe and forced his way in leading a stream of Frenchmen. Col. MacDonnell and his men managed to close the gates behind them and the garrison set about hunting out all of the Frenchmen who had worked their way in, killing them to the last man bar one drummer boy. Throughout the day the battle raged on around Hougoumont with French attacks being repulsed, but gradually the defenders began to run out of ammunition.

At 3:30 on the afternoon of 18 June Napoleon directed howitzer fire onto Hougoumont, which set the thatched roofs on fire. With the buildings burning down around them a message arrived for MacDonnell direct from Wellington ordering the troops not withdraw but to retreat into the gardens and continue to fight the enemy. Despite being surrounded and their defences burning down around them the Guards and Hougoumont held out for the battle. Matthew Clay and his defenders had been holed up for twelve hours of continual fighting but had survived the French onslaught.

Following Waterloo he returned home with the regiment and was promoted to Corporal in 1818 and sergeant in 1822. He later fought again in Spain during their Carlist Wars and upon leaving the army he joined the Bedfordshire Militia. Matthew died in Bedfordshire in 1873.

About 1:30pm whilst the Chateau was still under continual attack, 17,000 men of D'Erlon's Corps and 74 guns turned onto La Haye Saint in the centre to assault the left and centre of Wellington's line. With the French artillery pinning the Allies down on the ridge, Wellington ordered his men to move back behind the ridge and lie down to minimalize their casualties.

At 2pm Marshal Ney's (Napoleon's second in command) columns advanced on La Haye Saint, which was held by the King's German Legion. Like Hougoumont, La Haye Saint would sustain prolonged attacks by the French.

With Hougoumont and La Haye Saint occupied, the remaining columns moved onto the Allied centre, as they reached the crest of the ridge the British troops stood up, poured well-timed volley fire into the French and charged them back down the hill.

Somerset's heavy cavalry were ordered to charge the broken French columns and scatter them from the field to prevent them regrouping. Whilst the cavalry were successful in scattering the French infantry they overstretched themselves, as they were prone to do and continued to charge the French artillery. Now strung out and out on a limb, the French *cuirassiers* (French heavy cavalry) returned the charge and began to attack the British cavalry who were overwhelmed and had to fight their way out. Fighting in the ranks of the Lifeguards were two Cossall individuals, John Shaw and Richard Waplington. Waplington, born in 1787, had been working in the coal mines of the area since the age of 13, and stood at six feet tall, he joined to find a better way of life whereas Shaw, an apprentice carpenter in Radford, had previously helped to build the décor for Wollaton Hall, joined in October 1807 aged 18 due to a falling out with his Master. Both Shaw and Waplington enlisted together at

The Nottingham Goose Fair in the 2nd Life Guards, an elite cavalry regiment where only the tall and strong could serve. Owing to their hardened occupations prior to joining, both Shaw and Waplington became known for their height and strength throughout their regiment as the 'Cossall Giants'. Shaw especially, weighing in at 15 stone and standing over 6 feet tall, was a well known pugilist who had made money from prize-fighting and looked set to have quite a productive career in the Household Cavalry where prize-fighting prospered.

During the Waterloo Campaign the Household Cavalry found themselves taking part in several charges and counter charges, often involving French *cuirassiers*, their French heavy cavalry equivalent, but ultimately more terrifying to face owing to the fact they rode heavy horses and wore steel helmets and breastplates. It was during one of these charges later in the afternoon of 18 June that Shaw, who had killed many opponents on the field already, and had received a fair number of wounds himself, broke his sword whilst grappling with a group of *cuirassiers*. Never one to give up in a fight, Shaw removed his helmet and used it as a club to beat back the enemy, (reports claimed he took down nine enemy troops) until eventually he was shot from the saddle. Shaw was later found lying on a dung heap, evidently having died from his many wounds gained that day, and was buried at La Haye Saint, the British held farmhouse come fortress, in the days following the battle. Waplington, almost capturing himself a French Eagle was imminently overrun with French *cuirassiers* as he clutched the pole of the Eagle's standard and was cut down from his horse, never to be seen again. History can only speculate that he was buried in one of the mass graves after the battle, but was never named.

Elsewhere within the ranks of Somerset's Heavy Cavalry Brigade, Sir Arthur Benjamin Clifton (1771–1869), of the revered local aristocracy, was Lt. Col. of the 1st Royal Dragoons. The 1st Royals already had experience of fighting the French and had landed in Portugal in 1809 where mostly for their time in the Iberia they skirmished with French cavalry patrols on the Spanish/Portuguese border. They were used to cover the army's retreat to Busaco and Torres Vedras in 1810 and 1811 and again used to harass the French rear-guard as they pulled back into Spain. Following the winter retreat of 1811 they then followed Wellington's army as it advanced into the heart of Spain and took part in the engagements at Fuentes d'Onoro, Vittoria and the Pyrenees. Though present at the battle of Toulouse the regiment did not see action and following Napoleon's abdication they sailed home for England. When Napoleon escaped from Elba the regiment was despatched to Belgium in May 1815. Though they saw no action at Quatre Bras they helped cover the retreat of the allied army back to Waterloo. On 18 June the 1st Royal

Dragoons took part in the charge against d'Erlon's corps, where Captain Clark and Corporal Styles succeeded in capturing a French eagle of the French 105th Regiment. The 1st Royals lost 97 men and 97 wounded at Waterloo. Following the battle they returned to Dover in January 1816. Sir Arthur Clifton, leading his regiment in their many charges that day also reputedly took command of the brigade late in the afternoon of 18 June after their commander was wounded.

Thomas Wheatley, hailing from the same village as Shaw and Waplington was also playing his part on the field. A cavalryman also, Wheatley, a stocking weaver, joined the 23rd Light Dragoons in 1807 following an incident which involved him attempting to shoot his own father when he tried to break up a stocking weavers strike with which Wheatley was a sympathizer. Though it is not known exactly when Wheatley joined the 23rd, they had already seasoned their skills fighting the French in Spain where they had arrived in June 1809 and within a month engaged the enemy at Talavera in July of that year where their ranks were decimated after they charged into a dried riverbed and cut to pieces by the French. The 23rd Light Dragoons would not see enemy action again until April 1815 when during the Waterloo Campaign, under the command of Lt. Col. Earl of Portington and numbering 397 strong they charged bravely at both Genappes and Waterloo incurring 77 casualties.

Wheatley, surviving the Waterloo Campaign returned with the 23rd in December 1815 and left the regiment to become a blacksmith at Babbington colliery. Wheatley's military life did not stop with the 23rd, he joined the Nottinghamshire Militia and in 1832 he helped to defend Wollaton Hall against the mobs that had already attacked and burned down Nottingham Castle and Beeston Mills. Despite living quite a varied and stirring life, Wheatley died in poverty in Cossall Almshouses and was buried in Cossall churchyard.

At 3:30pm as the thatched roofs of Hougoumont were set alight, the King's German Legion holding La Haye Saint ran out of ammunition and soon the garrison fell to the overwhelming French numbers.

With La Haye Saint now in French hands Ney from his position saw British troops moving to the rear. Assuming that the British were in retreat Ney ordered two cavalry brigades to harass them. As the cavalry swarmed over the ridge they found, not the British troops in retreat, but carefully arranged into squares with artillery positioned intermittently. As the rear ranks of the French cavalry pressed up the ridge the horses at the summit had no choice but to press down into the valley where the British squares and artillery lay in wait. The cavalry was virtually decimated and Ney, unable to see the slaughter committed more cavalry to the attack until at 5:30pm when the attacks petered out. Later in the battle Henry

Paget, Earl Uxbridge, Wellington's second in command and cavalry commander was hit below the knee by artillery fire. He was carried to the rear where his leg was amputated.

Carrying Uxbridge's messages around the battlefield was Thomas Wildman, a young officer of dragoons acting as aide-de-camp to Uxbridge. Wildman joined the 7th Light Dragoons in 1808 as a Cornet and later that same year was promoted to Lieutenant. Wildman's role at Waterloo put him in certain danger of being hit by enemy fire and would bring him into close contact with the French positions. When Uxbridge was hit, Wildman was one of the first to attend him and helped to staunch the blood flow before carrying him to a surgeon's post. Wildman's bloodstained glove can be seen on display at the National Army Museum in London. Following Waterloo, Wildman bought Newstead Abbey from his childhood friend Lord Byron in 1818; two years earlier he bought a Majority in the 2nd West India Regiment and then the 9th Light Dragoons. He became a Captain in the Nottinghamshire Yeomanry in 1828 and after was promoted to Colonel in 1837 and Lt. Col of the 5th Dragoon Guards in 1840.

Elsewhere on the battlefield, 19-year-old William Green of Pixton, Mansfield was serving as a Driver in the Royal Horse Artillery having joined in 1813. He is recorded as serving as a wagon driver aged 19 two years later at Waterloo with George Bean's 'D'

Troop, RHA. Bean's troop at Waterloo were armed with five six pounder cannons and one heavy 5.5 inch howitzer. Bean's troop was positioned to the right of Wellington's line to alleviate pressure on Hougoumont from the massing French forces to assault the chateau. Supporting the infantry, the RHA Troops saw prominent action at Waterloo and were called upon to harass the enemy movements and break their advance. Green, as a driver in the RHA would have the dual role of not only ensuring the guns were in position where needed, but also that a constant supply of ammunition was present and the guns were maintained, often coming close to the enemy throughout the battle.

Following Waterloo, Green stayed with the RHA as a career soldier. His travels took him to Ireland where he met and married Catherine Kelly (Keely) in 1819. Green stayed with the RHA until 1836 when he left the army aged 40 and qualified for the Chelsea pension as well as being awarded the Waterloo Medal and the Service Medal. Following his army career, Green returned to Selston and later censuses record him as working as a labourer and having nine children. Green died in March 1877 aged 80 and was buried in the parish church of St Helen's, the same church he was christened in. Green's headstone can be seen today in the ground of the church.

Ney sent for reinforcements and Napoleon engaged his Imperial Guard, whom he had been keeping in reserve to the battle. The

Imperial Guard were Napoleon's elite troops who had seen action in all of his battles across the globe.

The Imperial Guard were despatched to the right flank to crush the garrison of Hougoumont and sweep over the ridge. However General Maitland's Guards units whom were lying down in the fields away from the supressing French artillery fire were ordered to stand by Wellington and deliver fire on the Imperial Guard. Taking the French completely by surprise, suddenly British infantry began springing up out of the ground and begin firing on the Imperial Guard. At this time the 52nd Light Infantry wheeled round and began to fire on the Imperial Guard's flanks forcing them back onto themselves. The Guard, completely shocked, halted, wavered and began to fall away and retreat from the field.

Wellington signalled for the whole allied force to pursue the broken French troops, some did stop turn and give fire but it was too late, the French army had been scattered and broken, Waterloo had been won by the Allies.

Throughout the battle the 2/59th were stationed to the tiny village of Hal on the extreme right of Wellington's army to block the main road linking Paris and Brussels. Owing to their position the 59th saw no action on June 18th, as other British battalions became embroiled in one of the most prolific battles in British military history, the 59th held off a group of about 5,000 cavalry who were scouting to find a route around the British line. Unfortunately as the 59th played no real part during the Waterloo Campaign they were later unable to count it as a battle honour.

In the days following Waterloo however the 59th was to lose some casualties to the pockets of resistance still holding out during the army's retreat. As they had suffered no casualties during the actual battle this meant that the 59th was one of the few regiments considered to be full strength and therefore placed at the head of the army as it advanced into France on 22 July 1815.

Cambrai in northern France made to hold a defiant stand. The British attacked headed by the 59th who easily overran the French positions but lost five men in the process. On 5 July Paris was in sight and the 59th camped to the north of the city. Whilst peace negotiations were being carried out in the city both armies were still facing a standoff with each other. The 59th lost yet another soldier when a sentry from the 59th's camp and a French sentry across the canal separating Paris from the British took pot shots at each other with the Englishman coming off worse. This incident took place only a few days before peace was officially declared making the 59th man one of the last soldiers of the Napoleonic War to be killed.

With peace declared the 59th was billeted at Montlhery until December 1815 when they were once again boarded onto transports at Calais where they were taken to Dover and then back to Ireland. Sadly, many of those serving in the 2/59th who had seen the final days of Napoleonic France met a disasterous fate when embakring onto troop transports HMS Seahorse and HMS Lord Melville were caught in a storm in Tramore Bay, Ireland on 30th January 1816. Of the 303 officers and other ranks, 33 women and 38 children, aboard the Seahorse only 28 men of the 2/59th survived. The Lord Melville was grounded but not wrecked, however, they still suffered 13 casualties of which 2 were soldiers of the 2/59th. This maritime tragedy had depleted the ranks of the battalion worse than any action against the French. With war now over and no need for a full time army, the decision was made that same year to disband the 2nd battalion of the 59th regiment instead of trying replace those lost.

The 45th however, were still boarding their troop transports when the battle of Waterloo commenced and ultimately remained in Ireland. They had embarked on one of the greatest campaigns registered in British military history and had fought in an army that is reckoned to have been the best yet fielded. By 1815 though, the 45th were able to boast the following battle honours:

Roleia, Vimiero, Busaco, Talavera, Fuentes d' Onoro, Cuidad Rodrigo, Badajoz, Salamanca, Vittoria, Pyrenees, Nivelle, Orthez and Toulouse.

CONCLUSION

Both the 45th and the 59th Regiments of foot witnessed some of the most prolific actions of the Peninsular War from 1808–14. The 45th were amongst the first 12,000 troops to land in Portugal and see Wellington's early victories, taking part in the brutal sieges of Badajoz and Cuidad Rodrigo and saw the final push back into France. The 59th took part in the harsh retreat to Corruna, the infamous Walcheren Campaign that almost destroyed the army, and the siege of San Sebastian. Between both regiments they saw almost every campaign of the Iberia. Interestingly enough, both regiments missed the Battle of Albuerra in 1811, where almost every regiment taking part suffered 40% – 50 % casualties and was the bloodiest engagement of the Peninsular War.

For nearly seven years both the 45th and 59th made up the backbone of Wellington's forces, standing shoulder to shoulder and firing well-timed volleys into the French ranks, choking on the acrid smoke, with faces blackened by powder and shoulders bruised from the kick meted out by their trust Brown Bess muskets. They never faltered; they never turned their backs on the enemy. They often fought weary, hungry and exhausted but somehow always stood their ground and pushed back the troops of the far superior French empire that faced them.

Even without both regiments present in the thick of the fighting at Waterloo, the county still had experienced and courageous Nottingham men in all spheres of the battle from the defence of Hougoumont, the heavy cavalry charges and the desperate reliance on the artillery to keep up a fast rate of consistent fire throughout the day to keep the once more superior forces at bay.

Whether they fought with the local regiments or in other units on the field one thing is clear, the men of Nottinghamshire were not to be cowed by the French war machine and would bravely take what was thrown at them to make their counties proud.

ACKNOWLEDGEMENTS

Since the conclusion of the Napoleonic War on the field of Waterloo in 1815, there have been many excellent works that record and recollect the entirety of the War in the Peninsula and the knowledge collected has amounted to volumes. Two such works are of course Napier's *History of the War in the Peninsula and South of France from the Year 1807 to the Year 1814* and of course Sir Charles Oman's *The History of the Peninsular War.* Both of these works could be argued as being the 'father' of writings on the Peninsula Campaign. They have provided a rich fountain of knowledge and dedication to the subject in question and most historians today would agree that at some point their context has been used again and again for the purpose of works to come.

There have been many notable Napoleonic historians in the decades following Napier and Oman that have written many extensive papers, theories and works on the subject of the Napoleonic War and the Campaigns in the Iberia. Those whose names spring to mind and have had major impacts in shaping how this work is researched are Michael Glover's *The Peninsula War 1807–14*, Roger Parkinson's *The Peninsula War* and Ian Fletcher's *Wellington's Regiments*. All of these historians have researched extensively the campaigns and actions of the Peninsula War and have painstakingly followed the actions and tribulations of The British Army and her allies as they slogged it out, advancing and retreating, with their French nemesis through three countries in the space of seven years.

Then there are the historians we must thank for their focus and detail to attention in bringing to us the life of the soldiers of the period, the social structure that they operated under, but also how they lived, fought and died. Thanks must go out to historians such as Philip Haythornthwaite for his life long works in this area, namely, *The Armies of Wellington, Weapons and Equipment of the Napoleonic War* and *Wellington's Military Machine*. Other authors who must also receive credit for their services to this field are Rory Muir for his intrepid *Tactics and Experience of Battle in the Age of Napoleon* and Robert Bruce's *Fighting Techniques of the Napoleonic Age*.

Of course, Wellington's progression during the Peninsula

was a mixed bag of pitched battles, sieges and defences. He had a professional army under his command that could not have operated as successfully as it did without the discipline and co-operation that became integral to its success. This force consisted of line infantry, artillery, cavalry, light infantry, siege artillery, the commissariat and wagon train, drivers, farriers and blacksmiths; the list goes on. A debt of gratitude goes out to such authors as Frederick Myatt for his outstanding book *British Sieges of the Peninsular War* for excellent insight into the trial and tribulation that befell the forces in trying to seize a fortification. We must also remember the work of Stephen Summerfield, Antony Dawson and Paul Dawson, and also Kevin Kiley for their work in assessing and analysing the power and potential of artillery during this era and its importance in ensuring the outcome of success in battle.

Other areas that have helped to provide research for understanding how Wellington's army in the Peninsula had managed to become one of the finest fighting forces that England has ever dispatched to a conflict are resources that enable us to determine the progression of the British army in general before, during and after its wars with France. Recognition for their hard efforts must go to Charles Messenger for his two works *History of the British Army* and *For Love of Regiment Vol 1*, and also the similarly named *History of the British Army* by Peter Young. Other works that have added to this already extensive knowledge but give excellent insight into the life of a redcoat soldier go to Richard Holmes' *Redcoat* and E.W. Sheppard's *Red Coat: An Anthology of the British Soldier during the last Three Hundred Years.*

Finally, we come to the source of this topic, the 45th Nottinghamshire Regiment. There has been very little work carried out on the specific topic of the 45th during the Peninsula War despite being one of Wellington's veteran regiments. However, of the work that has been done regarding the history of the regiment, the impressive analysis that is Phillip Hugh Dalbiac's *History of the 45th: 1st Nottinghamshire Regiment* and Col. H.C. Whylly's *History of the 1st and 2nd Battalions The Sherwood Foresters Nottinghamshire and Derbyshire Regiment 1740 – 1940 Vol. 1,* more than represents a well constructed history of the Midlands oldest regiment. I must also thank, A.S. Lewis for being one of the few authors I have come across who tells the story of the 59th (2nd Nottinghamshire) so well and for keeping their history alive with his excellent work *The Lilywhite 59th.* A special thanks also goes out to David Ingham for his specialist information and dedication into researching the 59th regiment.

A special debt of gratitude also goes out to Bryan Maloney and John Wheatley of Cossall Parish Council, Christine Dabbs, Stephen Seymour, and Mr. David Jackson. You all took a special interest in my *Nottingham at Waterloo* project to tell the story of the county's Waterloo heroes.

Finally, a last acknowledgement must go out to the staff and experts of the Sherwood Foresters Regimental Museum, Nottingham, for allowing me to use their resources and for providing much expertise and knowledge.

BIBLIOGRAPHY

Regimental Histories

Brown, Private William, *Recollections from a Soldier in the 45th,* (1829)

Dalbiac, P.H., *History of the 45th: 1st Nottinghamshire Regiment (Sherwood Foresters)* (Swan Sonnenschein & Co Ltd, 1902)

Fletcher, I., *Wellington's Regiments,* (Spellmount, 1984)

History of the 45th Foot, http://freespace.virgin.net/stephen. mee/45th_regiment.htm

Ingham, D., *Sudden Death, Sudden Glory - The 59th Regiment 1793 - 1830* (Jade Publishing, 1996)

Lewis, A.S., *The Lilywhite 59th,* (Blackburn Recreation Services, 1985)

Messenger, C., *For Love of Regiment: A History of British Infantry Vol. One 1660 – 1914* (Leo Cooper, 1994)

Ministry Of Defence, Regimental Histories

http://www.army.mod.uk/documents/general/45th_ Nottinghamshire_The_Peninsular_Burmese_Kaffir_Wars_and_ the_Abyssinia_campaign.pdf

South African Military History Journal Vol 4 No. 3 – 1973, *The History of the 45th regiments (The Sherwood Foresters)*

http://samilitaryhistory.org/vol043at.html

Whylly, Col. H.C., *History of the 1st and 2nd Battalions The Sherwood Foresters Nottinghamshire and Derbyshire Regiment 1740 – 1940 vol. 1,* (1929)

Housley, C., and Edwards, I., at *The Sherwood Foresters Regimental Museum Archives,* Chilwell Barracks, Nottingham.

British Army

Battles of the Nineteenth Century volumes 1-7, (Cassell and Company)

Haswell, J., *The British Army – A Concise History,* (Thames and Hudson, 1975)

MacFarlane, C., *The Great Battles of the British Army,* (George Routledge and Co., 1853)

Messenger, C., *History of the British Army,* (Bilson Books Ltd. 1993)

Sheppard, E.W., *Red Coat: An Anthology of the British Soldier During the Last Three Hundred Years* (The Batchworth Press, 1952)

The Peninsula War

Napoleon at War, (Osprey Publishing, 2002)

Esdaile, C., *The Peninsular War,* (London: Penguin Books, 2003)

Fitchett, W.H., *Battles and Sieges of the Peninsular War,* (London: Leonaur Ltd, 2007)

Glover, M., *The Peninsular War 1807-1814,* (Penguin Books, 2001).

Glover, M., *Wellington's Army in the Peninsula 1808-1814,* (London: David and Charles, 1977).

Myatt, F., *British Sieges of the Peninsular War,* (London: Guild Publishing, 1987).

Parkinson, R., *The Peninsular War,* (Hart-Davis MacGibbon, 1973)

Rathbone, J., *Wellington's War: His Peninsular Dispatches,* (London: Michael Joseph, 1984)

Robertson, I.C., *Wellington at War in the Peninsula: 1808 – 1814 An Overview and Guide* (Leo Cooper, 2000)

Snow, P., *To War with Wellington: From the Peninsula to Waterloo,* (John Murray, 2011)

British Peninsula Army

Franklin, C.E., *British Napoleonic Field Artillery,* (Staplehurst: Spellmount, 2008)

Haythornthwaite, P., *The Armies of Wellington,* (London: Brockhampton Press, 1996)

Haythornthwaite, P., *Wellington's Military Machine,* (Staplehurst: Spellmount, 1997)

Holmes, R., *Wellington: The Iron Duke,* (London: HarperCollins Publishers, 2003)

James, L., *The Iron Duke: A Military Biography of Wellington,* (London: Wiedenfeld and Nicolson, 1992)

Kirkby, M., *Wellington's Guns: A study of His conflict with the Royal Artillery 1808 – 1815,* (Chester University Press, 2010)

Longford, E., *Wellington: The Years of the Sword,* (London: The Literary Guild, 1969)

Oman, C., *Wellington's Army 1809-1814,* (London: Greenhill Books, 2006: Originally Published by Edward Arnold, 1913)

Windrow, M., *The British redcoat of the Napoleonic Wars,* (Franklin Watts Ltd, 1985)

Napoleonic Misc.

Adye, Capt. R.W., *The Bombardier and Pocket Gunner,* (7th edition, London: Military History Whitehall, 1813)

Bruce, R.B., Dickie, Iain; Kiley, Kevin; Pavkovic, Michael; Schneid, Fredrick, *Fighting Techniques of the Napoleonic Age 1792-1815,* (London: Amber Books Ltd, 2008)

Dawson, Antony; Dawson, Paul; Summerfield, Stephen, *Napoleonic Artillery,* (Wiltshire: The Crowood Press Ltd, 2007)

Glover, M., *Warfare in the age of Bonaparte*, (Pen & Sword Military Classics, 2003)

Haythornthwaite, P., *Weapons and Equipment of the Napoleonic War*, (Dorset: Blandford Press Ltd, 1979)

Haythornthwaite, P., *The Napoleonic Sourcebook*, (London: Guild Publishing, 1990)

Howarth, D., *Waterloo: A near run thing*, (Glasgow: Collins Fontana Books, 1972)

Kiley, K., *Artillery of the Napoleonic Wars 1792-1815*, (London: Greenhill Books, 2004)

Luvas, J., *Napoleon on the Art of War*, (New York: The Free Press, 1999)

Muir, R., *Tactics and Experience of Battle in the Age of Napoleon*, (London: Yale University Press, 2000)

Rothenberg, G., *The Napoleonic Wars*, (London: Cassell & Co, 2000)

von Clauswitz, C., *On War*, (Hertfordshire: Wordsworth Editions Ltd, 1997)

ND - #0220 - 270225 - C0 - 234/156/7 - PB - 9781780915364 - Gloss Lamination